Contending for the FAITH

Contending for the FAITH

Heresy and Apologetics

by
Theodore Plantinga

PAIDEIA PRESS
Jordan Station, Ontario, Canada

Canadian Cataloguing in Publication Data

Plantinga, Theodore, 1947-
Contending for the faith: heresy and apologetics

Includes index.
ISBN 0-88815-066-0

1. Faith. I. Title.

BT771.2.P56 1984 234'.2 C84-099691-8

 Published by Paideia Press Ltd., P.O. Box 1000, Jordan Station, Ontario, Canada L0R 1S0.

Cover design by Gerrit V.L. Verstraete, Christian Communications Centre, Toronto.

ISBN 0-88815-066-0
Printed in Canada.

By far the greatest battle that Christians have to fight is that with the false brethren, and the fight is so hard because, although they are not Christians, they wish to be known as such. If they were willing to call themselves Pilates, Judases and Herods, that is, if they were willing to lay aside the name Christian, we would endure all the injuries they dared to bring upon us; war would cease and there would be peace between them and us. Since, however, they insist on being regarded as Christians, we must fight them and in no wise suffer them to speak and do with impunity what is not befitting Christians.

—MARTIN LUTHER,
Table Talk

For I do not make myself out to be any kind of saint, nor am I now contending about my conduct but about Christian doctrine . . . On this I take my stand. I can do no other. God help me. Amen.

—MARTIN LUTHER
at Worms

OTHER BOOKS BY THE SAME AUTHOR

Historical Understanding in the Thought of Wilhelm Dilthey
Rationale for a Christian College
Reading the Bible as History
Wait for the Lord: Meditations on the Christian Life
Learning to Live with Evil

CONTENTS

INTRODUCTION

I

SOME words are suitable for use in polite society, and others are not. Profane and obscene words fall into the latter category, and so do certain terms used to refer to uncomfortable subjects. One such subject is heresy. Although the belief that there is such a thing as "heresy" has played an important role in Western history, many people today are convinced that this term is outmoded and archaic.

Others aren't so sure. One theologian, who has recently drawn up an "agenda for theology," identifies heresy as the issue that is most avoided in contemporary theology: "The leading candidate for 'most ugly issue in theology today' is doubtless heresy. We avoid it like bubonic plague."[1] What we avoid so resolutely, to put the point more precisely, is not heretical teaching as such but the notion that there is such a thing as heresy.

One of the reasons for avoiding this subject is that ours is an age of anxiety. The nuclear sword has been hanging over our heads for decades, and the threat has not diminished. The thought of what might happen if a political conflict ever gets out of hand adds a tension even to lesser conflicts—including conflicts in the realm of ideas. We have learned that we must seek peaceful resolutions to our disputes. Even when we disagree with someone, we often preface our statement of criticism with words of solidarity: "I'm very much in sympathy with what you said, but . . ."

Although such tendencies are also taking hold in evangelical Christian circles, Christians have not forgotten that their faith has been the occasion for much dispute and strife in history. James I. Packer, an evangelical Anglican theologian, reminds us that ". . . it is the nature of the gospel to create controversy; and the vigour with which the gospel is spoken against is an index of the faithfulness and power with which it is being preached."[2]

II

If ever there was a preacher who refused to compromise to avoid controversy and who preached the gospel with vigor, it was Martin Luther (1483-1546). But Luther and his time have become something of an embarrassment to us. We still celebrate certain Reformation themes and observe Reformation Day on October 31, but we tend to regard Luther with a mixture of fear and fascination. A leading church historian has characterized Luther's time by saying: "Men cared enough for the faith to die for it and to kill for it."[3]

Are there still Christians today willing to kill and be killed for the faith? There seem to be a few, but we hardly feel inclined to commend them for it. Most Christians are ashamed of the hostility and violence between Catholics and Protestants in Northern Ireland. And few Christians praise Islam for the militant spirit demonstrated by many Near Eastern Arabs in their hostility to the Jews in Israel and to the "Christians" in Europe and North America.

The religiously inspired battles of our time bring back memories we would prefer to see buried, memories of a time when much of Europe was involved in wars of religion, a time when Catholics and Protestants seemed eager to outdo each other in ferocity. In his book *Battle for the Mind* William Sargant observes:

> Neither Catholics nor Protestants can claim to have a cleaner record than their opponents. There was little to choose, for savagery, between the Protestants and Catholics in the German religious wars; Catholic massacres of the Jansenists and Huguenots in France were no less fanatic than the massacre of Irish Catholics by Cromwell's Protestants. Moreover, both Catholics and Protestants have carried the sword of God with equal vigor against the heathen overseas; and against members of the pre-Christian witch cult of Europe; always acting in the firm conviction that they were inspired by the highest and noblest motives.[4]

III

Against the background of two world wars, we have learned to look back at the wars of religion with new eyes. What sorts of people were those religious leaders of earlier ages who freely wielded the sword in the name of Christ's Kingdom? German scholars, especially, have been interested in possible connections between religious motivation and neurotic personalities. The historians and psychologists who try to figure out what made Hitler go so far astray also have their doubts about Luther, who, like Hitler, was the most influential German of his time. Could there be an "authoritarian personality" underlying the fanaticism of these two historical giants? Did Luther help pave the way for Hitler?

Embarrassed by Luther's aggressiveness in promoting the faith, theologians today are beginning to interpret the gospel in ways that leave conflict and divisiveness out of the picture. The United Presbyterian Church, in drawing up its "Confession of 1967," made "reconciliation" central. In a commentary on this confession we read that this term ". . . can epitomize the whole gospel in one word."[5]

What about all the language in Scripture that has to do with conflict and warfare? Christians used to love the hymn that begins: "Onward Christian soldiers, marching as to war . . ." And the church on earth was referred to as the "church *militant*" (to be distinguished from the "church triumphant" in heaven). It is now suggested that such military language should not be taken seriously, that it represents an accommodation to the time in which the Bible was written. Roland Bainton explains: "The use of military metaphors was a part of the Romanizing of the gospel. The Oriental understood what it was to bear the cross. The Roman responded better if told 'to fight the good fight.' "[6]

Another factor in the deep desire to avoid conflict is the commitment to "pluralism." Many people use this term today without knowing quite what they mean to say, for the term has many meanings, not all of which are compatible with one another or with the Christian faith. For most people who use the word, it stands for a gentle form of relativism that was simply unthinkable in Luther's time. The popularity of pluralism is regarded as a sign that modern man has "arrived." John Macquarrie observes: "Pluralism is taken to be the mark of a modern society as distinct from a primitive one. It could even be said that the index of a society's maturity is its pluralism, its capacity not only to tolerate but to maintain and even to encourage the existence within its bosom of diverse groups of people." Does this mean that the traditional Christian claim to absoluteness or exclusive truth is to be given up? Macquarrie apparently thinks so: "The nineteenth-century ideal of the conversion of all nations to the Christian religion, preferably in its Western and Protestant form, is a thing of the past. As far as we can see, there will be religious pluralism on this planet and that is probably a good and healthy state of affairs . . ."[7]

IV

Contemporary Christians who think along these lines and then look back to the Reformation era like to observe that the Anabaptists were "right." What they mean is that the Anabaptist refusal to use the sword to advance the cause of the church and the Kingdom of Christ is a position that has won out almost completely in Protestant circles today. We are sometimes left with the impression that Menno Simons (1492-1559) and his followers in the "left wing" of the Reformation were early adherents of today's sophisticated tolerance and gentle relativism. Weren't the Anabaptists the ones who maintained that service comes first while doctrinal differences are of little importance?

Not quite. When it comes to excommunication (another one of those ugly terms that theologians today are often ashamed to discuss), the Anabaptists had a highly developed view, and also a long history of putting their view into practice. Menno Simons left no doubt about the necessity of excommunication in certain circumstances:

> . . . it is evident that the congregation or church cannot continue in the saving doctrine, in an unblamable and pious life, without the proper use of excommunication. For as a city without walls and gates, or a field without trenches and fences, and a house without walls and doors, so is also a church which has not the true apostolic exclusion or ban. For it stands wide open to every seductive spirit, to all abominations and for proud despisers, to all idolatrous and willfully wicked sinners, yes, to all lewd, unchaste wretches, sodomites, harlots, and knaves, as may be seen in all the large sects of the world (which however pose improperly as the church of Christ).[8]

And he did not mean to exclude doctrinal offenses: false doctrine or "heretical, unclean doctrine" was a ground for excommunication.[9]

In the time of the Reformation, then, the Catholics, Lutherans, Calvinists, and Anabaptists were all on guard against heresy and regularly took steps to combat it. There was certainly disagreement on the nature of the weapons that could be used in contending for the faith, but that strong measures against heresy were called for was recognized by nearly all. The mentality of Erasmus (ca. 1466-1536), the great apostle of tolerance in the days of Luther, had not yet won much acceptance.

V

From my subtitle it is apparent that I mean to deal with both heresy and apologetics. I do not regard these as two completely separate topics. J. Gresham Machen asks: ". . . if we are to have Christian apologetics, if we are to have a defence of the faith, what kind of defence of the faith should it be?" He answers his own question as follows: "In the first place, it should be directed not only against the opponents outside the Church but also against the opponents within."[10]

Machen distinguishes here between enemies *outside* and *inside* the church. But as the church and the world live on side by side generation after generation, this distinction becomes harder and harder to draw. After all, where do the heretics get their mistaken notions? Very often those notions come from without, from non-Christian or anti-Christian sources and traditions. Thus the apologist's effort to defend the faith in the face of intellectual objections from non-Christian circles cannot be entirely separated from the systematic theologian's task of spelling out exactly what Scripture and the church teach in opposition to the deviations that arise *within* Christian ranks. Sometimes the defense of the gospel in the face of unbelief as it manifests itself within the church is a much more urgent concern than the continuing debate with thinkers outside the church who take an interest in the question of God.

It is not just in our century that the heretics within the church have drawn sustenance and support from philosophical and religious conceptions alien to the Judeo-Christian matrix within which the Bible arose. Hence we read in a history of apologetics that ". . . the infant Church carried out its apologetical encounter with Judaism, with paganism, and with deviant tendencies that arose within the Christian community."[11]

In our secular world, the battle for the gospel is essentially *one* battle. Western Europe and North America have been exposed to the gospel for so many centuries now that we can no longer distinguish clearly between unbelief outside the church on the part of people who have never heard the gospel, and apostasy within the church on the part of people who are forsaking the Word of God and giving their hearts and minds to other "gospels." The spiritual enemies outside the church have long ago infiltrated the Christian camp; in some places they have even taken over. We must recognize that a Humanist annexation of Christianity is underway in our time.

VI

The spiritual struggle in which Christians today are involved, then, is not just a battle for the Bible but also a battle for the church—indeed, a battle for the very soul of the Christian faith. If we are to discuss this battle, however, we must know what Christianity is and is not. In other words, we must deal with the question of definition (Part I). If the faith is to be defined, it must be by reference to some standard or ultimate authority. Christians have not always agreed on what that authority is (Part II). Once we have a final authority to appeal to, we can seek to determine what heresy and orthodoxy are and relate them to the diversity that will always exist, and also to the inevitable disagreements on matters of secondary importance (Part III). Finally, there are some neglected questions to take up. In our individualistic age we pay little attention to the nature and rights of institutions and organizations. We will see that Christian integrity in doctrine and conduct is not just a norm for individuals but also has implications for institutions and for the Christian community in general (Part IV).

PART ONE

THE PROBLEM OF DEFINITION

THE presupposition of this book is that the faith is worth fighting for. Those who love the Christian faith will also defend it when the need arises. But if we are to defend the faith, we must know what it is. How is the true faith to be distinguished from counterfeit versions? One might attempt to determine what the essence of Christianity is inductively by surveying its manifestations, but this procedure involves certain difficulties (Chapter 1). The other way to find out just what the faith to be defended is—and is not—is to trace its growth and development in history. As believers over the ages defended the faith against attack from within and without, Christianity defined itself in history (Chapter 2).

CHAPTER ONE

DEFINING THE FAITH INDUCTIVELY

I

FOR the past generation or so, many Christians have been uneasy about the church's identity. All around them they saw changes. Little reassurance was available as they sought to interpret events: the changes were greeted with enthusiasm by both Christian and secular journalists, and this added to their anxiety. Is the church still the church? Is the Pope still Catholic? Such were the questions that began to arise.

Arthur Herzog gave expression to what was running through many minds when he wrote:

> Already the Episcopal Church has abandoned the notion of heresy, which would seem to indicate that there is little to be heretical about. If it comes to pass that the Pope is not infallible, even in matters of faith and morals, if bishops are elected by popular vote, if priests can marry and nuns serve only a few years before departing to raise families, how will one define the Roman Catholic Church? How will a Catholic be different from a Protestant? How will the Protestant Church, having jettisoned the supernatural, prayer, authority in moral matters, and so on, having committed itself to liberal social causes, differ, say, from Americans for Democratic Action? Why should the individual join one rather than the other? And what *would* a Jew be?[1]

It seemed that the historical forms of Christianity were collapsing, perhaps to be replaced by a general religiosity or some sort of civil religion tailored to uphold the political order. Will Herberg, who has traced the convergence between Catholic, Protestant and Jewish religiosity in the United States, quotes the late President Dwight D. Eisenhower as saying: "Our government makes no sense unless it is founded in a deeply felt religious faith—and I don't care what it is."[2] The civil religion to which many Americans look as the source of consensus in American life has been described by Herberg as follows:

> I want to make it clear that when I designate the American Way of life as America's civil religion, I am not thinking of it as a so-called common-denominator religion; it is not a synthetic system composed of beliefs to be found in all or in a group of religions. It is an organic structure of ideas, values, and beliefs that constitutes a faith common to Americans as Americans, and is genuinely operative in their lives; a faith that markedly influences, and is influenced by, the professed religions of Americans. Sociologically, anthropologically, it is *the* American religion, undergirding American national life and overarching American society, despite all indubitable differences of ethnicity, religion, section, culture, and class. And it is a civil religion in the strictest sense of the term, for, in it, the national life is apotheosized, national values are religionized, national heroes are divinized, national history is experienced as a *Heilsgeschichte*, as a redemptive history.[3]

The notion of a connection between Christianity and political order goes back many centuries. A social and political religiosity in which the church champions and gives its blessing to the existing order is certainly one of the forms which Christianity has assumed in history. This type of religiosity is sometimes called the Christianity of the churches, which is then to be distinguished from the Christianity of the sects. The churches represent a Christianity that is at peace with its environment, a Christianity that has come to power, while the sects represent a Christianity that is alienated from the world and from the political order. Which of these two lines, which have coexisted throughout much of Western history, represents genuine Christianity? This question does not admit of a simple answer. And the situation is complicated by the fact that various groups which started out as sects gradually developed into churches at peace with the world around them.

The ability of institutional Christianity to develop and to maintain some sort of identity through change is one of the marvels of history. The discovery during the eighteenth and nineteenth centuries that much more change had in fact taken place than anyone realized is one of the reasons for the various cynical interpretations of Christian history, many of which are still with us today. But it also gives rise to the quest for "original Christianity." Louis Auguste Sabatier, writing in the nineteenth century, observed:

> Now, during the eighteen centuries of its history, Christianity has taken so many and such various forms, it has received so many developments in every sense, it has become a thing so rich and luxuriant, that it is far from easy to discover beneath this thick growth of institutions, dogmas, ceremonies, and devotions the tap-root of the tree from which it all has sprung, and from which it still derives its nutrient.[4]

II

The problem one encounters in defining Christianity and in tracing its source is paralleled in the investigation of other cultural phenomena. One might ask, for example, just what philosophy is. There is much disagreement on this score. One of the most influential answers is Whitehead's suggestion that it is a series of footnotes to Plato, or commentary on Plato's thought, taking the form of both criticism and further development. If this view is correct, we could regard philosophy as a long discussion that began among the ancient Greeks and has been going on ever since. The Academy founded by Plato continued to operate for more than 900 years, and many other philosophers and schools joined in the discussion as well.

The weakness of this thesis becomes apparent when one asks where this leaves the great thinkers of the Orient, for it seems to define them right out of the philosophical arena. Since their discussion of the great questions does not have its roots in Plato and the Greeks, it is not philosophy and therefore would not have to be studied in our colleges and universities. This is indeed the treatment generally accorded the thinkers of the Orient.

What the problem of the Oriental thinkers demonstrates is that there is often something arbitrary about our definitions. If we had begun by surveying the great thinkers of the East and the West to see what they have in common, we would not have come up with Whitehead's notion of philosophy as commentary on Plato. And when we turn to the question of the relation between philosophy and religion, we see again how arbitrary definition can be.

The problem might be posed by asking whether there can be a

Christian philosophy. For many thinkers a Christian philosophy would be a contradiction in terms: philosophy, we are told, accepts the authority of reason alone. We might grant that the Greeks indeed moved in such a direction and wished to regard man as the measure of all things, but we could still go on to ask whether a Christian philosophy in which God's revelation is the ultimate authority would not be an improvement upon—and development beyond—Greek philosophy.

Again, the definition is all-important. There is nothing contradictory about the notion of a Christian philosophy—unless we *define* philosophy as recognizing only reason as authoritative. If we do settle on such a definition, many great thinkers of the Middle Ages, as well as various philosophers of our time, will have to be expelled from the ranks of the philosophers.

Philosophers are not averse to expelling or excommunicating one another. Although we live in a pluralistic age, there are still philosophers who are quick to say of certain opponents that they are not "real philosophers." They call them historians or theologians or perhaps journalists. Not surprisingly, the philosophers who get the roughest treatment are the ones who call the philosophical tradition into question in the most radical manner. Here I think especially of Martin Heidegger, who is surely the most controversial philosopher of the twentieth century. Many philosophers of our time respect Heidegger deeply, but some dismiss him as a quack who hides his lack of genuine insight behind obscure, incomprehensible language. So fundamental is his proposed reorientation in philosophy that a great many philosophers find themselves unable to understand what he is talking about. (It must be admitted that some of them have not really tried either.) Should philosophy be defined in a manner broad enough to include Heidegger?

III

There is no standard answer to the problem of how philosophy is to be defined. Generally speaking, we recognize as philosophers people who regard themselves as such, who identify themselves with the philosophical tradition and write scholarly works which they brand philosophy.

We tend to do the same thing when it comes to defining the

term *Jew*. When Hitler was in power, the definition of this term was no academic question: whether or not one was classed a Jew was a matter of life or death. Today a Jewish person can claim certain rights in relation to the state of Israel which are not available to non-Jews. But what is a Jew? Again, an inductive approach would do little good. George W. Forell observes:

> The question, "Who is a Jew?" has never been answered to the satisfaction of Jews or non-Jews. At present, most Jews would be willing to grant that a Jew is a person who accepts himself as a Jew. The situation among Christians has become very similar. A Christian is a person who accepts himself as a member of this communion. All other human criteria have become ever more difficult to apply. And the same holds true for the confessional groups within Christianity.[5]

Forell's suggestion that a Christian is simply someone who regards himself as such is not a new one. It became important earlier in our century in the controversy between the fundamentalists and the modernists. The fundamentalists claimed that the modernists were not Christians and should therefore leave the church voluntarily. The modernists refused to leave, insisting that they, too, were Christians. But what did they mean by the term? Shailer Mathews, who participated in the controversy on the side of the modernists, explained simply that ". . . Christianity is only the abstract term for the beliefs and practices of Christians."[6] It is "the religion of people who call themselves Christians."[7] John Hick, who takes essentially the same approach, informs us: "Christian belief consists in the beliefs of Christians . . ."[8]

Such statements should not surprise us, for Christians of the liberal variety have long insisted on their right to define—if only for themselves—what the Christian faith means. In fact, the notion that each individual has the right to do his own defining is central to the modern outlook. James Hitchcock writes: "Modern culture is at its very root hostile to the act of definition and prefers an endlessly fluid reality, capable to being endlessly manipulated to serve the purposes of history."[9]

Some centuries ago, any suggestion that individuals may decide for themselves what Christianity is and may define the faith as they see fit would have sounded arbitrary and anarchical, but more recently we have been under the growing influence of nominalism, a philosophy that in effect denies essences and regards the process of definition as flexible, as tied to practical concerns. A classic expression of the nominalist approach to definition is the statement made by Humpty Dumpty in Lewis Carroll's *Through the Looking Glass:* "When *I* use a word, it means just what I choose it to mean—neither more nor less."[10] If Humpty Dumpty were a modernist, he would surely have no qualms about calling himself a Christian! And he would probably agree that Calvinism is the way of thinking of people who choose to call themselves Calvinists.

IV

As we continue to search for a definition of Christianity, we see that the line between what is Christian and what is not Christian is growing ever vaguer. We are accustomed to thinking of Christianity as one of the religions of the world— indeed, as the true religion—but various thinkers, especially because of the influence of Karl Barth, *deny* that Christianity is a religion. They tell us rather that it is the enemy of all religion. We are warned that religion can all too easily turn into spiritual self-sufficiency: "Religion and church membership may thus well become a kind of defense that the conventionally religious man throws up to protect himself against the absolute demand of faith."[11]

There are other such puzzles. The New Testament warns strongly against schismatics and false teachers, but many Christians, especially those who claim to be engaged in "mission work," are busy erasing the line between the church, which is charged with the task of proclaiming the gospel, and the world, which is to be called to repentance and conversion. In a critique of current approaches to mission Peter Beyerhaus observes:

> . . . world history as such is understood as the result of God's mission, and in the transformation of the social structures we are told to realize the features of the coming kingdom of God. From here the conclusion is not far off that historical engagement as such is already mission, i.e. the participation in the *missio Dei* in world history . . . Church and mission are leveled down to the dimension of the world. In such a concept the eschatological kingdom of Christ is swallowed up by the immanent achievements of historical evolution. Even if such evolution is ascribed to the work of the anonymous Christ, we are nearer to the monistic philosophy of history of Hegel and Karl Marx than to the prophecies of the Bible.[12]

The notion of the "anonymous Christ" and of "anonymous Christians" is central to much of the confusion about how Christianity is to be defined in our time. If Christ is active in a hidden way in the world, working among people who do not know His name or seek the fellowship of His people, Christianity could conceivably embrace the entire human race.

The notion that all men will ultimately be saved, which theologians call universalism, has been with us for centuries as a minority position. It is in our time that certain consequences—or perhaps presuppositions—of this position are being worked out. If many are saved without acknowledging Christ, what are we to make of their role in history? Are they hindering the establishment of Christ's Kingdom, or are they working in their own unknowing way for the realization of divine purposes? Here we are reminded of what Hegel called the "cunning of reason": he maintained that despite the opposition and conflict we seem to see in history, there is steady progress (a "historical evolution") toward the goal set by history (or "reason"). The actors on the historical stage serve reason's purposes without knowing it.

Such an outlook has interesting implications for how Christian unity is to be understood. If Christ is present even in secular people and forces and institutions, our ecumenical efforts should not be limited to Christian circles. John Macquarrie therefore calls for "secular ecumenism."

> . . . the basis for this ecumenism is not a nicely worked out ecclesiology or even a doctrine of redemption but simply that natural morality which is common to all men by virtue of their humanity. The Christian members of the group do not even forcibly baptize the others by calling them "anonymous Christians" or anything of the sort. It is enough that they are human beings . . . This type of ecumenism therefore comes as a timely reminder that the end of history, according to Christian belief, is not the church but the kingdom of heaven, and this is a more inclusive concept, gathering up both church and world in an eschatological unity. Our primary aim should not be the unity of the church. We look beyond that to the unity of mankind.[13]

There was a time when Christians spoke of the "visible" church and the "invisible" church. By the visible church they meant God's people on earth as organized in institutional form, while the invisible church was made up of all the true believers, both on earth and in heaven. Today, because of the new way of thinking, theologians are beginning to speak of a different kind of "hidden" or invisible church, a church made up of people who do the work of Christ without knowing His name. Dorothee Sölle explains:

> In Christ God has made us free, broken down the boundaries so that the official Church is no longer the only place to seek and believe in Christ. Isn't the "Church outside the Church" simply a consequence of secularization, a hidden Church, in which Christ is present unrecognized as on the road to Emmaus?
>
> Wherever people have to do with Christ, there is the hidden Church. They may not be ecclesiastically or even consciously having to do with him, but he is present anonymously.
>
> It is through the preaching of this very Gospel that the world has been transformed and become secular, and this means that Christ is also preached and believed where his name is never mentioned.[14]

What is going on in this line of thinking is that Christianity ceases to oppose secularization but embraces it instead, even taking credit for it! Hans Küng writes: "Surprisingly enough, Church and theology have not only—in the end—come to terms with the secularization process, but—particularly in the years since the Second Vatican Council—have even entered vigorously into the swing of it."[15] If the church, in the eyes of some, has ceased to be anything, it may be because it has become virtually everything—all things to all men!

V

It would appear from a survey of the contemporary Christian world, then, that little is to be established through an inductive procedure. To distil the essence or common denominator of all that now calls itself Christian or is called Christian seems well-nigh impossible. In short, an inductive method will not do. But the problem with an inductive approach does not arise solely from the confusion in which we now live. Herman Bavinck, writing early in our century, already warned against an inductive approach to the question of the essence of Christianity, arguing that it would not succeed in settling this issue any more than it had managed to distil for us the essence of religion when used by the proponents of comparative religion.[16]

The problem with an inductive approach is that it *presupposes* a criterion by which it is determined what is included in the survey and what is not. If we take an inductive approach to the problem of philosophy's essence and include Christian philosophers among the thinkers surveyed, it will turn out that philosophy is compatible with religion. But if we use a narrower sample in our survey, a sample that does *not* include Christian philosophers, we will get the opposite result.

If we are to establish the essence of Christianity by way of a survey, some weighty questions will have to be settled first. Do we recognize "anonymous Christians"? Do we recognize sects and cults that have sprung up on the fringes of Christianity and have incorporated certain elements of Biblical revelation into their scriptures and teachings? The decisions made on such questions will determine whether we come up with a broad or inclusive definition of Christianity, as opposed to a narrow or exclusive definition.

VI

We would also have to face squarely the painful question of false teaching. It is significant that the New Testament tells us that false teachers come in the name of Christ.[17] Hence we are not simply to take every prophet or theologian at his word when he claims to be a Christian.

In effect, the issue of nominalism comes up here again. In other words, can I make words mean exactly what I want them to mean? Do I have the right to call myself whatever I please? Is it the right of every citizen to declare himself a spokesman for Christianity?

Perhaps an example can help us here. Suppose an economist who claimed to be a Keynesian proceeded to contradict every one of Keynes's major economic theories. When challenged he might present long, complicated arguments about the proper interpretation of Keynes's views in today's economic circumstances. Keynes himself is no longer with us to protest, but wouldn't the time come when economists dismissed such a person as an imposter—in effect, a false teacher? And if so, isn't it conceivable that some theologians today are also false teachers, that is to say, interpreters who have twisted and distorted the Christian gospel beyond recognition? Are we obliged to construct a definition of

Christianity broad enough to cover even their peculiar version of the faith? I don't believe so.

To get at the question of the proper definition of the faith, we must look at history and the church. Christianity has not manifested itself first and foremost in history by means of individual human beings but rather by means of the church, of which Christ's disciples were the first leaders. And the church defined the faith in history, carefully setting it off from various false teachings that arose to challenge it. This process took centuries; it was not a matter of hasty decisions. Thus, even though Scripture remains the final authority for Christian doctrine, the church with its creeds has formulated Scripture's message. We will now investigate how central Christian doctrines were clarified and refined in history.

CHAPTER TWO

DEFINING THE FAITH IN HISTORY

I

IF a definition is to be effective and useful, it must be specific. And if it is specific, it will necessarily be exclusive. If we define the word *Canadian*, for example, in a manner that allows human beings of all nationalities, regardless of where they live or whether they have ever set foot in Canada, to qualify as Canadians, our definition will not be of much use, for it will exclude no one from citizenship and the voting list.

This point does not apply solely to the work of scientists, government officials, and people who make dictionaries. Institutions must also be able to define themselves by way of exclusion; otherwise they will eventually stand for nothing whatsoever. The Christian church today, as we have seen, must decide whether it wishes to be regarded as part of the process of secularization that has given us twentieth-century Humanism. The church, in brief, must define itself.

If the church does so, it may have to exclude from its fellowship some people who wish to participate and belong. The issue is then on whose terms they are to participate—their own, or the church's. Painful and unpopular measures sometimes have to be taken.

The early church found itself in a situation that parallels today's situation in many respects. Although there was plenty of confusion and disagreement, the church pursued a cautious policy that eventually had the effect of excluding certain groups. Marcion, a major thinker of the second century and a man of considerable influence, was among those who were excluded. It seems that there was an "anti-ecumenical" spirit abroad in the early church, and it began with the apostles, who issued strong warnings against false teachings and those who promoted them.

II

The period in which the early church spread beyond Palestine throughout the Mediterranean world was an age of syncretism or synthesis. There was much interest in religion, but the religious thinkers of the time were distinctly ecumenical or broad-minded. With Greek and Latin available as international languages, nations which had long lived in isolation from one another were beginning to discover each other. The Greek mind was being combined with the spirituality of the Near East. There was room for Judaism in the new synthesis, and also for the followers of Jesus Christ.

In short, the early church quickly found itself confronted with rival faiths which sought to swallow it up, just as today certain elements of Humanism seem interested in absorbing or annexing Christian movements and institutions. The church could not long delay its response to this situation—hence the warnings against false teachers issued by the apostles.

The greatest threat to the church came from the philosophical and religious thinkers known as the Gnostics. Paul Tillich characterizes them as follows:

> The Gnostics were not a sect; if anything, they were many sects. Actually, however, gnosticism was a widespread religious movement in the late ancient world. This movement is usually called syncretism. It was a mixture of all the religious traditions of that time. It spread all over the world, and was strong enough to penetrate Greek philosophy and the Jewish religion . . . Hence, gnosticism was an attempt to combine all the religious traditions which had lost their genuine roots, and to unite them in a system of a half-philosophical, half-religious character.[1]

It was not a foregone conclusion that Christianity would resist the lure of the Gnostic synthesis and try to keep itself pure. For many students of church history, it is far from clear what pure and original Christianity is—and whether it includes the spirituality of the Old Testament as exemplified in the psalms. (There is the problem of the psalms of imprecation, for example.) Adolf Harnack, who has spoken of Christianity as "the syncretistic religion *par excellence*,"[2] views the development of Christian doctrine as a mixture involving a simple, pure gospel and alien influences. Gnosticism, he explains, was a movement in the direction of a "world-religion"; the notion of the unity of mankind was much in the air. Christianity did not seem to be universalistic in the same sense as Gnosticism, but of course the gospel could be reinterpreted. Harnack explains the proposed synthesis as follows:

> The Gospel was recognized as a world-religion only in so far as it could be severed from the Old Testament religion and the Old Testament, and be moulded by the religious philosophy of the Greeks and grafted upon the existing cultus-wisdom and practice of occult mysteries. The means by which this artificial union was to be brought about was the *allegorical* method as used long since by the Greek religious philosophers. The possibility of the rise of a Christian gnosticism lay in this, that the Christian communities had everywhere fallen heir to the heritage of the Jewish propaganda, where there was already an exuberant tendency to spiritualize the Old Testament religion, and where the intellectual interest in religion had long been unbridled.[3]

The Christians did not all agree on how to respond to the Gnostic challenge and the issues it raised. In the first couple of centuries, thinkers associated with the Egyptian city of Alexandria (e.g. Origen, Clement) favored a synthesis with the Greek mind, especially the philosophy of Plato, which paralleled Gnosticism in some significant respects. But in the end the Gnostic forces did not win out, even though it must be admitted that their influence has never been entirely outgrown in the church's history. It was gradually recognized that what Gnosticism stood for simply is not identical—or even compatible—with the Christian gospel. James Orr observes: "That the triumph of Gnosticism, notwithstanding the germs of truth in some of the higher systems, would have meant the dissolution of historical Christianity and certain ruin of the Church, is granted by writers of nearly every school."[4]

III

It is significant that the church responded to these challenges comparatively slowly and was careful not to issue arbitrary statements in an effort to get disagreements settled in a hurry. We see this deliberate caution reflected in the long-standing disagreement on the New Testament canon: it was not until the fourth century that it was agreed which books make up the New Testament scriptures. On this point, and on others, the church learned to live with a measure of uncertainty and confusion.

The early church was famous for its doctrinal disputes. People sometimes wonder whether so much theological hair-splitting was necessary, but such an attitude results mainly from ignorance. The fact of the matter is that the church was well aware what the central question is; the debate was not over the number of angels that can dance on the head of a pin. Herman Bavinck writes: " 'What think ye of the Christ?' is and remains the main question in religion and theology."[5] He even identifies it as the "question of the ages."[6] It was around this question that the doctrinal disputes revolved.

Bavinck also observes that ". . . Jesus was not the first Christian; He was and is the Christ. He was not the subject, but the object, of religion."[7] Hence the church did not seek to probe the "self-understanding" of Jesus, as various modern scholars have tried to do. Since Jesus was being incorporated into rival religions (just as today He is given a place in Mormonism and in Islam), the church tried to spell out what it means that He was God incarnate—the Son of God, but born of a woman.

Many of the early doctrinal controversies, then, concerned Christology. Arising out of Gnosticism with its disdain for the flesh and the realm of matter was the Docetic heresy, which was a denial that Jesus was truly human. Taking its name from the Greek word for appear or seem (*dokeo*), this conception of Christ in effect made a charade of His ministry among us and His atoning sacrifice: it was argued that Jesus only *appeared* to suffer on the cross, or sometimes that the man who was crucified was someone other than Jesus.

The early Christians rejected the Docetic interpretation of the Christ event as undermining the very basis of the Christian understanding of redemption. Some of the affirmations in the creeds should be read with the Docetic heresy in mind: the Apostles' Creed, for example, assures us that Jesus "suffered under Pontius Pilate" and that He really did die, for it mentions explicitly that He was buried. The first verse of I John may also have been written against the background of the Docetic heresy: "That which was from the beginning, which we have heard, which we have seen with our eyes, which we have looked upon and touched with our hands . . ."

A similar heresy confronted by the early church was Apollinarianism. Once again the divine nature of Christ was emphasized so strongly that insufficient place was left for His human nature, as though Jesus was a divine mind in a human body. This position was strongly criticized by the church fathers, who perceived that a redeemer who was not fully man would not be an adequate savior. The Apollinarian position, too, was clearly excluded in the creeds that were eventually formulated.

The most famous of the Christological heresies was Arianism, which was named after the fourth-century theologian Arius, who went too far in the opposite direction. Arius maintained that Christ or the Word was created. He did not claim that the Son of God was only a man, for he made Him the first of all created things and instrumental in the creation of the world. But the Father alone was eternal and unbegotten, according to Arius.

The great opponent of this position was Athanasius, whose thinking eventually won out and was declared orthodox. The issue was formulated in terms of the question whether the Son is of "one substance" or the same essence (Greek: *homoousios*) with the Father. The Arians said no to this formulation and maintained that the Son is of a "similar substance" (Greek: *homoiousios*) with the Father. This was a weaker position, but, as has often been noted, there was only an iota (the Greek letter "i") of difference between the two formulations. The Athanasian position triumphed at the Council of Nicea in 325. In the Nicene Creed, which is officially endorsed by many churches today, we read that the Son is "begotten not created, of the same essence (*homoousion*) as the Father."[8]

IV

These great battles, I fear, are little understood today. Church history is not a popular subject. Few Christians have any idea what was really at stake. G. K. Chesterton, who speaks of the "thrilling romance of Orthodoxy," sheds some light on what he calls those "monstrous wars about small points of theology." Balance and precision were needed to avoid the pitfalls in the church's path: "To have fallen into any one of the fads from Gnosticism to Christian Science would indeed have been obvious and tame. But to have avoided them all has been one whirling adventure . . ." Chesterton was keenly aware that ideas have consequences. Therefore firmness was called for:

> The Church could not afford to swerve a hair's breadth on some things if she was to continue her great and daring experiment of the irregular equilibrium. Once let one idea become less powerful and some other idea would become too powerful. It was no flock of sheep the Christian shepherd was leading, but a herd of bulls and tigers, of terrible ideals and devouring doctrines, each one of them strong enough to turn to a false religion and lay waste the world.[9]

Somewhere in the midst of all this controversy scholars locate the birth of dogma, the officially proclaimed teaching of the church. Dogmas are not opinions or mere theories or intellectual fads, and they should not be proclaimed when there is no need for them. They are formulated in response to a situation, a specific need. Dorothy Sayers explains: ". . . dogmas are not a set of arbitrary regulations invented *a priori* by a committee of theologians enjoying a bout of all-in dialectical wrestling. Most of them were hammered out under pressure of urgent practical necessity to provide an answer to heresy."[10]

Some theologians, however, view the development of dogma in darker terms, as a series of false additions. John Hick, for example, speaks of the "deification of Jesus" and argues: ". . . it is extremely unlikely that Jesus thought of himself, or that his first disciples thought of him, as God incarnate." We do not know very much about "Jesus' self-understanding," according to Hick.[11]

The important question is whether there is support in Scripture for the Christological decisions and definitions of the early church. However one might choose to answer this question, it is clear that the New Testament writings for the most part present Jesus against the background of the Old Testament promises and prophecies. What is implicit and not clearly spelled out in the Old Testament becomes manifest in the New. The same relation of implicit to explicit is often used to defend the development of Christological dogmas in the early church. Such a defence is certainly in order, but it does not wholly account for the development of dogmas and doctrines. Heresy and the threat of syncretism also play a role here.

V

The concept of orthodoxy, then, cannot simply be equated with the explicit teachings of the New Testament. It was the church that determined what orthodoxy is as she defined the faith in history. What should amaze us is not that so much strife was required to achieve these results but that the faith as defined has stood for so long. Robert A. Kraft sums up the grand development as follows: "By the year 400 of the common era, there had developed what can be called 'classical Christian orthodoxy.' This type of Christianity became mainstream Christianity in both the eastern and western world prior to the time of the Protestant Reformation."[12]

It is important to note that these main doctrinal lines defining orthodoxy do not rule on every conceivable theological issue. The church spoke officially when necessary and excluded certain views as incompatible with the gospel, but it did not seek to be theologically comprehensive or exhaustive. The dogmatic decisions concerned the very heart of the faith. Jaroslav Pelikan observes: ". . . the only dogmas in the most precise sense of the word are the dogmas of the Trinity and of the person of Christ, as these were defined in the first four (or seven) ecumenical councils."[13]

The central question for religion and theology, as we have seen, is: "What think ye of the Christ?" It is this question that is addressed in the formulation of dogma. Many of the early controversies involved the two natures of Christ. Settling this question required discussing the relation of the Son to the Father, and also to the "Spirit" of whom we read so much in the New Testament. Thus the Christological issue led naturally to the formulation of the doctrine of the Trinity.

This dogma as developed by the early church does not correspond directly to any one passage of Scripture. It has sometimes been argued that the doctrine of the Trinity simply is not taught in Scripture, and in at least one sense this seems to be the case. Yet the church found it necessary to formulate such a doctrine so that believers could be protected against false and misleading conceptions of Christ.

That the church took these matters with the utmost seriousness is apparent especially from the Athanasian Creed (which, despite the name, was not formulated by Athanasius). In this creed we read: "Now this is the Catholic faith, that we worship one God in Trinity and Trinity in unity, without either confusing the persons or dividing the substance." The bulk of the Creed is made up of complicated trinitarian formulations that are not suitable for use in worship services. The Creed is more theological than liturgical, but it is surely not theological in the sense that the points it makes are "merely academic." The Creed opens with these words: "Whoever desires to be saved must above all things hold the Catholic faith. Unless a man keeps it in its entirety inviolate, he will assuredly perish eternally." The closing words reinforce this point: "This is the Catholic faith. Unless a man believes it faithfully and steadfastly, he will not be able to be saved."[14]

When we read such strong words, we might wonder about the believers in Bible times. Did Abraham, Moses, David, Peter, and Paul hold "the Catholic faith"? Clearly not in this explicit form. But this need not concern us, for they did not confront the choices faced by the Christians who lived during the days of the Athanasian Creed, when there were so many different conceptions of Christ between which one had to choose. The same point could be made with regard to children who are believers: children face fewer choices. In short, the challenge of heresy made doctrinal definition and self-consciousness a necessity. Here we see in part what it means that the faith is defined *in history*.

VI

If Christian orthodoxy has taken shape and been defined *in history,* we must seek to understand it historically. But what does this mean? Thomas Oden gives us part of the answer when he argues that ". . . Christianity has a right to be understood historically, as it has understood itself, even as every individual person has a right to some degree to be judged not merely in terms of his present momentary transgressions, but in terms of his larger lifelong intentionality and long-standing behavior patterns."[15] In other words, the Christian faith must never be identified or equated with specific persons, episodes, errors, and so forth, which is what some people are inclined to do in rejecting Christianity as the oppressive religion of their youth. Christianity has a 2000-year history and must be understood in terms of that history, not in terms of an infinitesimal portion of it.

But historical understanding also involves a willingness to examine Christian affirmations and decisions *in context*. The British philosopher R. G. Collingwood can help us here with his "logic of question and answer." Collingwood argues:

> . . . you cannot find out what a man means by simply studying his spoken or written statements, even though he has spoken or written with perfect command of language and perfectly truthful intention. In order to find out his meaning you must also know what the question was (a question in his own mind, and presumed by him to be in yours) to which the thing he has said or written was meant as an answer.[16]

To get at the meaning of the dogmatic formulae regarding the Trinity and the two natures of Christ, we must find out what questions were in the minds of the church's leaders and thinkers when they were drawn up. This requires a commitment to serious historical scholarship.

But this historical emphasis can easily lead to *historicism*, that is, an absolutizing of the historical process in which no norms are applied to what history produces. We see a manifestation of historicism in the widespread complaint that traditional Christian theology is irrelevant because it offers answers to questions that modern man is no longer asking. The implication, of course, is that Christian theology should get better acquainted with modern man and seek to answer the questions he does have on his mind.

To argue along this line is to make history one's ultimate authority. It may indeed be true that modern man—unlike Martin Luther in the sixteenth century—is not greatly concerned with sin and guilt and being made right with God; he seems more concerned with liberation and autonomy. But does this mean, as some Christians seem to think, that Christianity should be reshaped in such a way as to maximize the "emancipatory possibilities" contained in its heritage? Must Christianity ask modern man what his needs and aspirations are and then define itself in such a way as to be able to meet them? Or must Christianity contradict modern man and tell him that he does *not* understand his own needs and that he must look to the Bible to find out who he is and what his true needs are? To do the latter would be to elevate the Bible above history as an authority for man and thereby to reject historicism.

The upshot of the matter is that we must distinguish between the notion that the faith is defined *in history* and the notion that it is history and its needs (i.e. the perceived needs of the hour) that must define the faith. When the faith is defined, it must always be by reference to some authority or authorities. We will see in Part II that there is disagreement on which authorities are to be used.

PART TWO

THE ISSUE OF COMMON GROUND

THERE is a good deal of disagreement about the meaning and proper interpretation of the Christian faith. If the disputes that arise are to be settled amicably, some sort of common ground must be found so that the various sides will have something to appeal to as they contend for their version of the faith. But is there such common ground? And if there is, is it common to Christians only, or is it shared with those who do not believe in Christ?

Throughout history a number of sources of religious authority have been proposed as the common ground for settling disputes. Some thinkers have interpreted the doctrine of general revelation to mean that reason is part of—or perhaps central to—God's revelation to man (Chapter 3). Others, also working with the notion of a general revelation, have emphasized our experience, especially of nature, as common and authoritative (Chapter 4). Virtually all Christian thinkers recognize Scripture as a court of appeal common to all who take the trouble to study it diligently and submissively (Chapter 5). But if Scripture is accepted as a central authority, the role of tradition, which is significant not just for Roman Catholics but also for Protestants, remains to be considered (Chapter 6).

CHAPTER THREE

REVELATION AND REASON

I

GOD'S revelation is not limited to the written Word. Virtually all major Christian thinkers have recognized that in addition to His special revelation or word-revelation God has given us what is usually called "general revelation." There is some dispute about the appropriateness of this contrast between "general" and "special" revelation, but the idea behind the notion of a revelation in nature or in creation is widely accepted.

What is the medium of God's general revelation? Various media have been suggested, and it is conceivable that general revelation might use more than one of them. In the next chapter we will consider the notion that general revelation comes to us through experience (broadly conceived); in this chapter we will look at the relation of "reason" to general revelation. As we shall see, it is a topic with a long history.

II

In order to say something about the relation of reason to general revelation, we must first try to determine what reason itself is. And this is far from easy. Julian Marias observes: "It would be hard to find a word with more divergent meanings than *reason*."[1] Nonetheless, some distinctions can be made.

For many thinkers, reason is a set of mental contents—perhaps a body of ideas or principles which all men have in common, given to them, presumably, by God. If so, reason might well serve as common ground in disputes about religious and theological matters.

Another conception is that reason is one of our faculties, to be distinguished from such faculties as will, desire, emotion, sensation, feeling, and imagination. (There are various different classifications of the faculties to be distinguished from reason.) A commitment to reason would then be a determination to allow reason, which is to be trusted, to guide one's conduct, and not to allow oneself to be swayed by other, less reliable faculties. This would open up the prospect of a rational approach to religion. The assumption, again, is that reason is universal, while other elements or aspects of man's make-up are individual or particular—and therefore potentially divisive.

A third conception is that reason is a tool or a criterion by means of which we evaluate whatever is proposed to us for our acceptance or belief, regardless of where it comes from. In such a view, other faculties (e.g. imagination) might generate ideas, but only reason would be competent to judge them. Here, too, reason could be conceived of as universal and therefore as representing common ground.

A fourth, less elevated conception of reason is that it is the power of logical thought and discrimination. This view does not presuppose that reason is the universal element able to bind men together, for it recognizes the possibility of different and conflicting principles of thought. Some philosophers insist on thinking along dialectical lines, for example, but many others reject dialectic.

The first three views of reason have been formulated somewhat abstractly: two of them are sometimes found together in a single thinker's conception of reason. We must remember that reason is one of the grand themes in the history of Western philosophy and that a great deal has been made to depend on it. It is precisely its centrality to so much of the philosophical tradition that makes it hard to define. The most important ideas (e.g. goodness, truth, justice, beauty) seem to escape definition in the ordinary sense. It might be argued that they are the elemental building blocks that make it possible for us to define other words of secondary importance. If so, we cannot define them in terms of those other words.

III

Reason is a central notion in the history of philosophy. Thus we find it emerging in Greek thought. The growth of the concept of reason among the Greeks is bound up with changes in their conception of the divine. Werner Jaeger observes: "In the western world, universalism began neither with the Christians nor with the prophets of Israel, but with the Greek philosophers." Thus universalism was in part the result of distrust in the traditional conception of the gods. "Since Homer's time," writes Jaeger, "the Greeks had come to recognize how various the ideals of the gods were among individual nations; and this realization could only lead them to deduce, from the very fact of this particularism, the vanity of all such distinctions between gods, however naturally they may have come about."[2]

As the Greek concept of reason grew and developed it became part of the concept of divinity. Anaxagoras, one of the early Greek philosophers, came to think of the mind as "the very essence of the Divine." Jaeger explains: "To Anaxagoras the Divine is pure reason—the activity of the Mind as taskmaster. Man has direct access to the Divine by similar powers that he bears within himself."[3] This notion was carried forward into the mainstream of Greek philosophy. E. R. Dodds tells us that for Plato, reason was "an active manifestation of deity in man."[4]

A commitment to the centrality of reason is usually combined with a distrust of other aspects of man's make-up. So it was with the Greeks. Dodds explains: "The Greek had always felt the experience of passion as something mysterious and frightening, the experience of a force that was in him, possessing him, rather than possessed by him."[5] In a study of the emergence of philosophy among the Greeks we read: ". . . throughout early Greek philosophy *reason* is acknowledged as the highest arbiter, even though the Logos is not mentioned before Heraclitus and Parmenides."[6]

The very significant role for reason in the philosophies of Plato and Aristotle was foreshadowed, then, in the lesser-known earlier philosophers. The full-blown conception of reason among the Greeks is summarized as follows by John F. Hayward:

> . . . if Reason is viewed in the honored station to which Plato and Aristotle assigned it, as capable of penetrating to Being Itself, and discovering the Essence of all things, then man takes on a godlike and ultimately secure status above the usual tides of human affairs by the mere exercise of his rational powers. Plato represents Socrates as believing that his life of Reason had prepared him for a blessed immor-

tality. Aristotle was bold enough to suggest that the fulfillment of "Theoretical Reason" put man into direct relationship with the reasonableness of Being itself, a reasonableness which he called "Thinking about Thinking," and which he attributed to God and man as a common power.

This powerful drive in Greek culture toward rational transcendence over the accidents of fate and fortune reached its climax in Plato and Aristotle and subtly wrought a major change in basic conceptions of reality. Under the triumph of classical Hellenic rationalism, the universe came to be regarded as essentially knowable and rationally ordered. The old fear of spirits and fate, of the uncontrollable and inscrutable, gave way to what was considered an enlightened conception of reality and of human existence.[7]

The implications for the history of philosophy and religious thought are not hard to discern. Reason is the divine in man; it is that which God and man have in common. Therefore human rationality can be regarded as inherently revelatory. John Baillie rightly observes: "Rationalism and the Speculative Method in theology are in no sense creations of the seventeenth and eighteenth centuries, but represent . . . a well-established tradition which goes back through the Middle Ages to the attitude assumed towards religion by the Greek philosophers."[8]

Given the conception of rationality as the link with the divine, it should come as no surprise that various Christian thinkers who were influenced by Greek philosophy had trouble conceiving of reason or rationality as subject to the corrupting effect of man's fall into sin. And if reason was essentially untainted by sin, it could serve as common ground. This way of thinking came under attack during the Reformation and again in the nineteenth and twentieth centuries.

IV

The Greek conception of reason laid the foundation for a "natural theology" based on general revelation alone. We see this way of thinking emerge clearly in Thomas Aquinas, who has exercised more influence on Roman Catholicism than any other thinker. Bernard Ramm writes: "The Roman Catholic position is that the general revelation of nature may be so read by man apart from Christ and apart from grace that he can prove that God is, and know some of his attributes."[9] Today there are many Catholics who feel uncomfortable with such a position. Yet for Aquinas, the notion of natural reason operating on its own was of great importance: it provided common ground in the debate between the Christian and the unbeliever. Ramm explains: "The philosophy of Aristotle as Thomas incorporates it into Christian thought becomes the basis of common ground for argumentation with the heathen. Natural reason is common to pagan and Christian alike and forms the court of appeal in religious debate."[10] It appears that Aquinas enjoyed doing battle with his opponents on *their* territory.

The outlook of Aquinas has remained the mainline position within Roman Catholicism. The Vatican Council of 1870 declared that the "Holy Mother Church holds and teaches that God . . . may certainly be known by the natural light of human reason, by means of created things."[11] Natural reason has been recognized as functioning especially in the domain of morality. John L. Thomas writes: ". . . Catholic thought has consistently vindicated man's natural ability to discover moral order and the norms for right moral conduct." Supernatural or special revelation is required in order to grasp certain central truths such as the Trinity and the incarnation, but ". . . unaided human reason is capable of discovering sufficient knowledge of general ethical principles to make judgments of value."[12]

V

The next step in the elevation of reason as the central religious authority took place in the context of the Renaissance. The Platonist tradition, which various Christian thinkers embraced and interpreted to mean that reason is the divine in man, was influential especially in the Academy at Florence. The philosophers of Florence, of whom Marsilio Ficino and Pico della Mirandola were the most prominent, advocated a syncretistic approach. Their goal, according to N. A. Robb, was "to establish rational bases for religion by showing how the witness of all philosophies pointed to the truth of the Christian revelation."[13]

The Platonist strand continues into subsequent centuries. Herbert of Cherbury (1583-1648) maintained that God provided all men with a common set of religious notions. Benjamin

Whichcote (1609-83), who was one of England's "Cambridge Platonists," identified reason as a direct revelation of God to the soul, arguing: "To go against reason is to be against God . . . Reason is the Divine governor of man's life. It is the very voice of God."[14]

The rational emphasis in religion also manifested itself in non-Platonist circles. A notable example is the English philosopher John Locke (1632-1704), whose deep aversion to what was then called "enthusiasm" was rooted in his conviction (shared with the Cambridge Platonists) that reason is the "candle of the Lord"[15] and ought to be our guide in our conduct.

In the seventeenth and eighteenth centuries, this confidence in reason led to a "natural" or rational religion (often called *deism)* that went well beyond Aquinas's natural theology. For Aquinas, supernatural revelation disclosed truths not available to natural reason, but for the adherents of rational religion, the Christian faith as based on special revelation was essentially a "re-publication" of what was already contained in natural religion. Matthew Tindal, one of the deists who held this position, summed it up nicely in the title of his major book: "Christianity as Old as Creation; or the Gospel, a Re-publication of the Law of Nature" (1730). It was Aquinas who had unwittingly and unintentionally paved the way for such a development. Hector Hawton observes: "To Aquinas, as to many of the Greeks, the Order of Nature seemed the expression of the divine reason . . . Thus we get the foundations on which Christian Rationalism was later built."[16]

The classic thinker in this mold is John Toland, the author of *Christianity Not Mysterious* (1696). The purpose of this book was to thoroughly harmonize the Christian faith with what reason allowed and demanded. Toland argued: ". . . *Reason* is not less from God than *Revelation*; 'tis the Candle, the Guide, the Judge he has lodg'd within every Man that cometh into this World."[17] God has ". . . endu'd us with the Power of suspending our Judgments about whatever is uncertain, and of never assenting but to clear Perceptions."[18] Since reason and Scripture both come from God they cannot clash, although they may on occasion *appear* to contradict one another. Are we then to suspend belief in what reason seems to be telling us? Toland writes:

> A seeming Contradiction is to us as good as a real one; and our Respect for the *Scripture* does not require us to grant any such in it, but rather

> to conclude, that we are ignorant of the right Meaning when a Difficulty occurs; and to suspend our Judgments concerning it, till with suitable Helps and Industry we discover the Truth. As for acquiescing in what a Man understands not, or cannot reconcile to his Reason, they know best the fruits of it that practise it. For my part, I'm a Stranger to it, and cannot reconcile my self to such a Principle.[19]

The upshot, then, is that reason must take precedence over Scripture. Joseph Butler, an Anglican bishop and the author of a highly influential apologetic work entitled *The Analogy of Religion, Natural and Revealed, to the Constitution and Course of Nature* (1736), argued along similar lines and made reason the standard by which to test and judge revelation.[20] Such was the "Christian rationalism" which had grown out of the Greek understanding of the divine by way of Aquinas's notion of a natural theology. The rational religion of Immanuel Kant had many forbears.

VI

Since the time of Toland and Butler there has been further movement in this direction. As we saw earlier (p. 23 above), some contemporary theologians conceive of Christian theology as part of the secularizing trend in our society. Hans Küng writes: ". . . Christians can be humanists and humanists can be Christians . . . Christianity cannot properly be understood except as a radical humanism."[21] José Porfirio Miranda, in a book on the "Christian humanism of Karl Marx," assures us that ". . . authentic Christianity means solid, unequivocal humanism."[22]

Humanism, in turn, must be viewed as a continuation of the Greek outlook with which we began this chapter. In a book on Humanism understood as "the Greek ideal," we read:

> The specifically Greek outlook proceeds from Homer onward like a broad highway, along an area covered also by secondary roads, and with tributaries debouching from or merging with the main road. Somewhere in the Roman period, to retain the image, secondary roads combined to cause a marked detour, which eventually, with Renaissance and humanism, gradually rejoined and merged with the main highway. Its character was inevitably altered, but in its outlines and direction it was unmistakably a continuation of the Greek way.[23]

Explicit Humanists like Hector Hawton speak language reminiscent of the Greeks. As he describes what held the various types of Humanists of our century together, he observes: "They were rationalist, in the sense that they put their trust in reason as a means of discovering truth and of settling disputes. They accept the discipline of using reason to explore the world . . ."[24]

In our century, of course, this Greek Humanism is to be encountered in a fully secular form. For the secular Humanist, reason is no longer what God and man have in common, for God is out of the picture. Yet it is still the highest in man and his guide in life's perplexities. Thus Humanism is not simply to be equated with atheism, for it is to be found among both Christians (i.e. Christian rationalists) and atheists.

VII

Christian rationalism has come in for a good deal of criticism over the years. Both Calvin and Luther protested against the excessive reliance on reason on the part of many Christians. Luther used strong language: ". . . Reason corrupted by the devil is harmful, and the cleverer and more richly endowed it is, the more harm it does, as we see in wise men who are led by their reason to reject the Word . . ."[25] Menno Simons differed with Luther and Calvin on a number of points, but he agreed on the danger posed by reason: ". . . human reason is in Adam so depraved through the bite of the old crooked serpent that it has kept but little which is conducive to godliness. Yet, it has become so perverse, haughty, ignorant, and blind that it dares to alter, bend, break, gainsay, judge, and lord it over the Word of the Lord God."[26]

James I. Packer clearly stands in the Reformation tradition when he warns against the assumption that ". . . the human mind, working by its own light, is the final arbiter of truth . . ." He points to the danger of pride and "intellectual impenitence." When the gospel calls us to repentance, the *mind* is not to be excluded. Packer writes: "Repentance means a change of mind; part of which, as we saw, is the abandoning of the sinful quest for intellectual autonomy and the recognition that true wisdom begins with a willingness to treat God's Word as possessing final authority. Repentance means renouncing the pride which would hail man as the measure of all things . . ."[27]

Various theologians of the twentieth century have attacked the infatuation with reason on the part of many Christian thinkers. The names of Karl Barth and Emil Brunner come to mind. One of the most thoroughgoing critiques of the rationalism inspired by the Greeks is Lev Shestov's book *Athens and Jerusalem*. Shestov claims that the warning to Adam and Eve not to eat of the tree of the knowledge of good and evil represents "the only true critique of pure reason that has ever been formulated here on earth."[28] Man, inspired by false rationalistic ideals, sought a knowledge that was not attainable:

> . . . man, seduced by the serpent, was not content with this knowledge: the "that" (*hoti*) did not suffice for him; he desired the "why" (*dioti*); the "that" irritated him just as it irritated Kant. His reason aspired avidly to universal and necessary judgments; he could not feel satisfied as long as he had not succeeded in transforming the truth that was "revealed" and situated above both the universal and the necessary into a self-evident truth . . .[29]

In his hunger for knowledge conceived of in rational terms, man refuses to *believe*, that is, to assent to givens of revelation whose truth is not self-evident for him. The first man ". . . also wished 'to know,' not 'to believe'; he saw in faith a kind of diminution, an injury to his human dignity, and he was certain of this when the serpent told him that after he had eaten of the fruits of the forbidden tree he would become like God—knowing."[30]

What Shestov calls for, then, is radical reconstruction in philosophy and theology. He does not propose to renovate the edifice of philosophy: he wants to begin with demolition. And the foundation, as we have seen, was laid by the Greeks. Shestov therefore argues: "We must, before everything else, reject the basic categories of Greek thought, tear out from our being all the postulates of our 'natural knowledge' and our 'natural morality.' "[31]

VIII

What Shestov advocates is not a total repudiation of reason in every form. He observes that ". . . those who have fought against reason have basically always fought against its immoderate pretensions."[32] The challenge, then, is to properly integrate reason into human life, without assigning it an undue role. What we call reason is indeed a marvelous gift of God, but it is not all-sufficient, as Remy Kwant notes: "Critical reason cannot explain in a purely rational way why a well-prepared meal is tasty, why the tender green of spring revitalizes man, why a certain angle of light improves the vista, why the beautiful pleases, why man and woman are attracted to each other . . ."[33]

Borrowing an analogy from the world of drama, we might say that reason is to play an important supporting role, but not the leading role. The philosopher David Hume (1711-76) surely was not an enemy of reason as such, but he recognized this point and therefore wrote: "Reason is, and ought only to be the slave of the passions, and can never pretend to any other office than to serve and obey them."[34] Although Hume's philosophy has been analyzed extensively, the full implications of his limitation of reason have not yet become widely apparent.

There is a definite place for reason in Christian life and thought, but not as the final court of appeal or as the screen through which everything must be filtered. Toland was wrong: the Christian faith *is* mysterious at heart. It is not only a stumbling-block to the Pharisees in their self-righteousness, it is also foolishness to the Greeks and to the proud Western intellectual tradition. Calvin, who is often called a relentless logician, was keenly sensitive to the foolishness of the gospel:

> Paul says that "the gospel is foolishness to the wise of this world" (I Cor. 1:18-20). And that is true, not only because its simplicity, which is popular and devoid of ostentation, is a laughing-stock to them, but also because it contains many things which, according to human standards, are irrational in the extreme—and ridiculous into the bargain! For the fact that the Son of God, who is life eternal, is declared to have put on our flesh and to have been a mortal man, the fact that we are said to have procured life by his death, righteousness by his condemnation, salvation by the curse he bore—all that is so greatly out of step with the common outlook of men that the more intelligent a man is the quicker he will be in repudiating it.[35]

Paul spoke from experience. When he addressed the philosophers in Athens, he found that Christ's resurrection from the dead is an offense to proud reason. Luke reports: "Now when they heard of the resurrection of the dead, some mocked; but others said, 'We will hear you again about this' " (Acts 17:32). Then, as now, intellectual pride stood in the way of repentance and conversion.

CHAPTER FOUR

REVELATION AND EXPERIENCE

I

THE notion of general revelation as common ground in the debate about religious and theological questions takes on various forms. Some thinkers who repudiate natural theology in the sense of the Christian rationalism of Toland, Tindal and Butler look to another faculty by means of which all men may receive divine revelation—feeling or personal experience.

The most important proponent of such an approach is the German theologian F. D. E. Schleiermacher (1768-1834). In an important apologetical work entitled *On Religion: Addresses in Response to Its Cultured Despisers,* Schleiermacher tried to present Christianity in a new light. He asked his hearers to disregard the dogmas and practices which most people had come to associate with Christianity. He then redefined and reworked the key concepts of Christianity in experiential terms in an effort to convince his hearers that religion is not distant and foreign but is part of modern consciousness rightly understood. There is a place for miracles in modern experience, he argued, and also for revelation:

> For me . . . everything is miraculous. For you what is inexplicable and strange is miraculous, but that is not what is meant by a miracle in my sense at all.
>
> The more religious you become the more of the miraculous you are likely to see all around you . . .
>
> What is "revelation"? Every new and original communication of the universe and its inmost life to men is a revelation. Thus every moment such as I have pointed out above can be seen to be revelatory, if you are properly conscious of its special character. But, in fact, every combination of perspective and feeling that has originally developed out of such a moment emerges as a revelation.[1]

Felix Flückiger has summed up the key insight in this approach to experience and revelation. What characterizes Schleiermacher's theology, he writes, is that he

> . . . equates the pious self-consciousness of the Christian with revelation. The elevated vitality of the spirit which we can encounter in the Christian church and which unites all Christians in a common elevated feeling of bliss is understood as divine being in us. The Spirit that worked powerfully in Christ is also working powerfully in us. Just as the self-consciousness of Christ was a revelation of God within him, so the pious self-consciousness of Christians is a revelation of God in us.[2]

Rudolf Otto, an admirer of Schleiermacher's approach to religion, speaks of the faculty of "divination," which renders us capable of "*genuinely* cognizing and recognizing the holy in its appearances." Schleiermacher in effect made use of this notion, Otto informs us. Thus there is a revelation of the holy in our experience. Otto writes:

> Religion is convinced not only that the holy and sacred reality is attested by the inward voice of conscience and the religious consciousness, the "still, small voice" of the Spirit in the heart, by feeling, presentiment, and longing, but also that it may be directly encountered in particular occurrences and events, self-revealed in persons and displayed in actions, in a word, that beside the inner revelation from the Spirit there is an outward revelation of the divine nature. Religious language gives the name of "sign" to such demonstrative actions and manifestations, in which holiness stands palpably self-revealed.[3]

II

For Schleiermacher and Otto there seems to be an affinity between art on the one hand and religious experience and feeling on the other. The Romantic notion of the sublime, as we find it in William Wordsworth, for example, comes to mind. Other theologians have pointed to moral awareness as an aspect of experience in which revelation seems to shine through. Abraham Kuyper writes: "Even without the Bible or nature you are already carrying a revelation of God around within you. This fact becomes apparent to you whenever your conscience accuses you after you have sinned . . ."[4]

The same point is made in a more picturesque manner by Benjamin B. Warfield, another Calvinist theologian:

> Conscience must be conceived, therefore, as a mirror hung in the human breast, upon which man may read the reflection of the divine judgment upon himself. When frowns of a just anger conceal his face, the clouds gather upon its polished surface: and surely when those shades pass away and the unclouded sun gleams once more from its surface, it cannot be other than the reflection of God's smile.[5]

III

Another way to develop the doctrine of general revelation without falling prey to Christian rationalism is through an emphasis on nature. The words *rational* and *natural* both function as normative terms: when a course of action is judged rational or natural, we mean that it meets with our approval. Thus, if we reject the notion that the "rational" is always to be interpreted as in accordance with God's will, we might still wish to say that what is "natural" meets with God's approval. This was the route followed by Tertullian, who is well known for his opposition to Greek philosophy and to any synthesis of Christianity with the Greek mind. Tertullian asked: "What has Jerusalem to do with Athens, the Church with the Academy, the Christian with the heretic?"[6] What is not as widely known is that he eventually left the church and founded a sect of his own.

Tertullian rejected "reason," but he put "nature" in its place. Nature can be known universally and without special revelation; it is itself a revelation. Arthur Lovejoy therefore observes:

> The anti-intellectualism of Tertullian and his hostility to the Greek philosophic systems have become so notorious as to overshadow the fact that, in a whole series of passages . . . he appears less as an Early Father of the Latin Church than an Early Father of the deism of the 17th-18th centuries, a precursor of Herbert of Cherbury, Toland, Tindal and Voltaire; certainly these could have found in him a rich store of texts suitable to be prefixed to their own writings.[7]

IV

The question that arises from such uses of the doctrine of general revelation is whether there is room for a knowledge of God apart from so-called special revelation. Many Christian thinkers have resisted this suggestion, while others have embraced it openly, arguing on the basis of Romans 1:19-20 that certain attributes of God are clearly apparent from an examination of the world around us.

Both sides point to passages in Calvin in support of their position. Although he stays away from the term *general revelation*, Calvin does talk about the issue behind the term in Book I of his *Institutes of the Christian Religion.* But his comments must be read carefully, for he does *not* endorse the view that the natural man can derive true knowledge of God from his experience of nature around him. He does write that there is ". . . no nation so barbarous, no people so savage, that they have not a deep-seated conviction that there is a God." What does he mean here when he speaks of "a God"? Does he mean a true knowledge of God, however faint? Clearly not, for a few lines later he assures us that ". . . even idolatry is ample proof of this conception."[8] A little farther on he writes that God

> . . . daily discloses himself in the whole workmanship of the universe. As a consequence, men cannot open their eyes without being compelled to see him. Indeed, his essence is incomprehensible; hence, his divineness far escapes all human perception. But upon his individual works he has engraved unmistakable marks of his glory, so clear and so prominent that even unlettered and stupid folk cannot plead the excuse of ignorance.[9]

Man is "compelled" to see, but God's "divineness" still escapes him. Calvin seems to give with the one hand and take away with the other. Does this mean that there can be revelation without the message getting across? This might sound strange, but a little reflection shows that it is quite well possible. Let us suppose that my son is undergoing a dangerous operation, and I am anxiously awaiting word of the outcome. Let us suppose further that the surgery is being performed in China by a doctor who speaks only Chinese. When the doctor comes to me to reveal what happened in the operating room, he may deliver his message in flawless Chinese, but it will mean nothing to me because I don't understand a word of Chinese. In such a case we could say that the message was clearly stated but that the person to whom it was addressed simply failed to comprehend it. In the example the barrier is purely linguistic, of course, but a spiritual barrier can also have the effect of blocking out what is communicated or revealed.

The point of Calvin's caution in relation to general revelation is that no room must be left for the construction of a natural theology, a theology based solely on givens other than special revelation, givens that can be properly interpreted by the natural man apart from faith and Christ. There is no such common ground between belief and unbelief.

We must be careful, however, not to discuss this issue too much on an intellectual plane, as though the unbeliever responds to general revelation solely and exclusively by failing to get the point. In a deeper sense he does get the point—and then stoutly resists it. Hendrikus Berkhof clarifies what is at issue here when he observes that "*mis*understanding is not the same as *not* understanding." We read in Romans 1 that ". . . God's eternal power and divine nature are clearly revealed to men, but they suppress the truth by worshipping and serving created things rather than the creator." Berkhof takes this to mean that ". . . one cannot simply say that God did indeed reveal himself, but that somehow it did not get through to man. On the contrary, man becomes guilty because something essential does reach him, something which he, however, cannot endure . . ."[10]

If general revelation is truly revelation, it cannot simply be ignored. Natural man cannot help but respond—and respond he does, by distorting and perverting its content. And this is precisely what makes the battle against the false faiths so painful and difficult: they contain glimmerings of the truth. The Canons of Dort, which function as one of the doctrinal standards of various Reformed churches, therefore speak of "glimmerings of natural light" or a "certain light of nature."[11]

V

This line of argument should not be understood as a complete dismissal of the notion of general revelation. It is not being suggested that what is called general revelation has no value as revelation. The question is whether it can function effectively as revelation *on its own*. Herman Bavinck observes soberly that "mankind has not found God by its light."[12] General revelation, if it is to function in the life of the believer, must be understood in the light of special revelation. Bavinck argues: "General revelation leads to special, special revelation points back to general. The one calls for the other, and without it remains imperfect and unintelligible."[13]

We should not regard this dependence of general and special revelation on one another as a result of the fall into sin, as though man would have been able to find God by means of general revelation alone if sin had not clouded the picture. Geerhardus Vos maintains that we must think in terms of a "preredemptive special revelation."[14] The integrating guidance of a word-revelation was already available to man in Paradise, helping him gain clarity about his place in the cosmos. And the covenant relationship between man and God called for specific word-revelation, such as the probationary command not to eat of the fruit of a certain tree.

General and special revelation are to be read in the light of one another, but it is special revelation, the revelation of Christ not just as our Redeemer but also as the second person of the Trinity through whom "all things were made" (John 1), that integrates the various dimensions and aspects of revelation and makes them truly comprehensible. Hendrikus Berkhof observes: "That Christ is *the* truth does not mean that there are no truths to be found anywhere outside of him, but it does mean that all such truths are fragmentary and broken unless they have become integrated in him as the center."[15]

VI

It could well be asked whether it even makes sense to separate these two aspects of revelation, for they appear to be intertwined in many ways. Elements of nature become signs in God's dealings with His people. The rainbow, which is a beautiful natural phenomenon, has a special meaning for us because it is a revelation symbolizing a promise of God made to Noah. Calvin, using the term *sacrament* to cover certain signs, asks: "And cannot God mark with his Word the things he has created, that what were previously bare elements may become sacraments?"[16]

Given such considerations, it should come as no surprise that various theologians object to the term *general revelation*. Hendrik Kraemer, for example, writes: ". . .'General Revelation' is a confusing term, because the content with which it is usually filled is a radical misrepresentation of what the Bible wants to convey." He complains that it ". . . is one of the most misleading and confusing terms possible and ought to be abolished."[17]

The exact nature of the contrast between general and special revelation is not easy to state. Theologians have sometimes spoken of a revelation in things (*revelatio realis*) as opposed to a revelation in words (*revelatio verbalis*), but this is too abstract an opposition, for God's special revelation to Israel involves a series of deeds or acts, such as the deliverance from Egypt.

Hendrikus Berkhof takes a firm position on this issue and suggests that *revelation* is too strong a term to use for the manner in which God might be known "in his works of creation." Berkhof writes: "We live by the revelation of God to Israel and in Christ." As for the other revelations, we should not speak of them as "general." Berkhof suggests: ". . . we might perhaps use words like 'partial,' 'groping,' 'dim,' unfulfilled,' etc. But all these terms, too, have their drawbacks, and they say very little."[18] Thus general revelation, like reason, ought to play a supporting role rather than the leading role.

VII

Many twentieth-century theologians are deeply suspicious of any attempt to construct a theology on the basis of a reading of the natural order apart from Scripture or special revelation. One of the reasons for this concern is the misuse of the notion of a general revelation by certain thinkers and church leaders within Hitler's Third Reich. The Barmen Declaration, which was formulated in opposition to the "German Christians" (i.e. the Christians who had compromised the gospel to accommodate the Nazis), therefore included a pointed rejection of any notion of a revelation outside the *Word* of God: "We repudiate the false teaching that the church can and must recognize yet other happenings and powers, images and truths as divine revelation alongside this one Word of God, as a source of her preaching."[19]

To disregard God's revelation in Christ is to stray from the path altogether, according to Herman Hoeksema: "A theology that ignores the revelation that has now come through Christ Jesus can never be any more than mere philosophy of man, always creating his own God and worshipping an idol."[20] And this observation in turn suggests a link between general revelation and heresy: one way to look at heresy is to regard it as an elevation of general revelation at the expense of special revelation, an elevation that leads to a grave distortion of the truth. The heretic makes his appeal to some authority other than Scripture (although he is usually willing to work certain elements of Scripture into his message). Benjamin B. Warfield writes: "The very essence of 'heresy' is that modes of thought and tenets originating elsewhere than in the Scriptures of God are given decisive weight when they clash with the teachings of God's Word, and those are followed to the neglect or modification or rejection of these."[21]

God's revelation in our experience or moral consciousness or in nature around us must not, then, be taken as common ground upon which unbelief and Christian faith can resolve their differences. Neither is it a court of appeal for Christians to use when they disagree about the meaning and import of Christianity. The court of appeal is rather the Word of God as we now possess it in written form. Hence we turn next to Scripture as revelation.

CHAPTER FIVE

SCRIPTURE AS REVELATION

I

THE conclusion to be drawn from the previous two chapters is that if God's general revelation by itself cannot serve as common ground for settling disputes about the meaning of the Christian faith, we will have to turn to His special revelation, that is, to the Word of God written—the Bible. Yet, although such a conclusion appears to answer an important question, it also gives rise to some new ones. Just what is the Bible? Theologians are by no means agreed on this matter.

Shailer Mathews, who participated in the fundamentalist/modernist controversy on the side of the modernists, argues that ". . . the Bible is the product and record of the first stages of the Christian religion . . ." In other words: "The Bible sprang from our religion, not our religion from the Bible."[1]

J. Gresham Machen, who was one of Mathews' opponents in the debate, criticizes such a view. In the conception of Christianity represented by Mathews and other such thinkers, he observes, ". .. all doctrines spring from life." Since Christianity is essentially a way of life for Mathews, life comes first and is then reflected in doctrine. Machen's own position is diametrically opposed to this: he maintains that Christianity ". . . founds morality upon truth, and life upon doctrine."[2] If Machen is correct the Bible cannot be simply a reflection of the church's way of life; in other words, it cannot be a product of the early church.

II

The issue behind the disagreement between Mathews and Machen can be further clarified by considering the familiar dictum that we ought to read the Bible in the same way that we read any other book. Mathews would of course agree with this statement, but Machen would not. The Bible, in Machen's view, is an unusual book in that as we study it we must distinguish between the primary author (God) and the various secondary authors (Moses, Luke, David, Paul, John, and so forth). In other words, the Bible was indeed written by human beings but was at the same time inspired by God and therefore serves as divine revelation to man. This confers upon the Bible an authority enjoyed by no other writing. The Bible is to be *accepted* as true and need not be *proven* true.

The liberal or rationalistic tradition has difficulty accepting this principle, for it requires that we agree to submit to the Bible as God's Word even *before* we have determined for ourselves just what it means to say. James I. Packer writes that theologians who think along rationalistic lines maintain that ". . . we must study the Bible as unbelievers before we are entitled to study it, or what is left of it, in a way consistent with faith."[3] In other words, the theologian must maintain a scientific neutrality and detachment; he may not bow to the Bible as the life-giving Word of God.

For such theologians, the Bible clearly does not function as ultimately authoritative: reason or scientific method does instead. If the Bible's claims are to be believed, they will first have to be verified by scientists and scholars. Hence Packer speaks of the "rationalistic passion to prove Scripture true."[4] The desire to see Scripture vindicated may be commendable, but the "rationalistic passion" underlying it is far removed from submission to the Bible as God's Word.

From the title of a controversial book that has sold widely, we know that there is a "battle for the Bible" underway.[5] In all the excitement the real issue is sometimes lost from view. According to Packer, the main concern in the "battle for the Bible" is "the detecting and rejecting of all principles which would undermine evangelicalism by making it impossible for the Bible to rule the church."[6]

III

The liberal or rationalistic undermining of the Bible involves a distinction that cuts right through the material making up the Bible. We are asked to distinguish that which is central to the Bible and worthy of acceptance from that which is peripheral and time-bound and not binding for us today. In other words, a distinction is made between kernel and husk, the central message and the package in which it comes to us. Rudolf Bultmann's program of demythologizing the Biblical message is an apt illustration of this tendency. In the words of Shailer Mathews, when the modernist approaches the Bible, he ". . . knows how to separate between the permanent and the temporary in its pages."[7] The "permanent" element is sometimes identified as the "substance," and the "temporary" as the "form."[8] In short, the Bible's content is permanent, while the form in which the content is presented may vary from age to age in the church's proclamation of the message.

The prospect of being able to distinguish between kernel and husk in the Bible has proven attractive to many theologians, including some in the orthodox camp. If Biblical authority were limited to the "kernel," the heart of the Biblical message, it might not be so difficult after all to defend the doctrine of the Bible's infallibility and/or inerrancy. (These two terms do not have the very same meaning, although the difference between them is hard to spell out; the latter term seems to stand for a more specific position than the former.)

When orthodox theologians approach Scripture in this way, they usually distinguish between what the Bible somehow implies or suggests or presupposes, on the one hand (e.g. that the earth has four corners), and what it *intends* to teach (i.e. how man is to be made right with God). The Bible's authority is then limited to the latter; in other words, it is to be believed and trusted in which it *teaches*, but not in everything on which it *touches*.

Another way to make such a distinction is to say that only the Bible's central saving message is authoritative—not all the historical details and injunctions about life in Bible times. Jack Rogers argues that *Christ* must always be kept in mind as the central interpretive principle of the Bible: "Scripture is not about everything. It is about Jesus Christ and the salvation he came to offer and effect."[9] Adherents of such an approach to Scripture like to emphasize that the Bible is not a history book[10] or a science textbook.

IV

In the case of certain theologians, at least, there are commendable motives behind such talk about Scripture, such as a healthy emphasis on the redemptive-historical character of the main line in the narrative. Still, there are definite dangers in this way of thinking. Machen therefore argues that it is "highly misleading" to say that "the Bible is not intended to teach science."[11]

Rogers, as we saw, claims that the Bible is not "about everything." This assertion requires careful examination. Since the Bible tells us about the origin of all things in God's activity as Creator and about the ultimate consummation of the historical process in the full establishment of the Kingdom of God, and also characterizes the time in between (i.e. the fall into sin, the old dispensation, Christ's atoning work and ascension to be seated at the right hand of the Father, and the nature of the new dispensation as the "day of salvation"), it is, in a very significant sense, "about everything," even though it is short on detail. But the relative lack of detail need not concern us. When we read a biography of Abraham Lincoln, we don't reject the author's claim that he has dealt with Lincoln's entire life simply because he has not accounted for each day!

We should be wary of any claim that the Bible is partial or incomplete. The Bible is complete in that it tells us about the creation, man's fall into sin, his redemption through the work of Jesus Christ, and the end of human history. Neither is the Bible partial in its inspiration or authority. The "Chicago Statement on Biblical Inerrancy" adopted by a group of evangelical Christians in 1978 warns against any attempt to dismember the Bible or break it up into parts, some of which may be more acceptable than others: "We deny that the inspiration of Scripture can rightly be affirmed of the whole without the parts, or of some parts but not the whole."[12] Scripture must not be played off against Scripture.

V

Among various theologians there is a fear that there may be "errors" in the Bible. Earlier generations of theologians seemed to take this issue more lightly. Charles Hodge, whose thinking is often dealt with as exemplifying an inerrantist position,[13] made the following memorable comment about the issue of errors in the Bible:

> The errors in matters of fact which skeptics search out bear no proportion to the whole. No sane man would deny that the Parthenon was built of marble, even if here and there a speck of sandstone should be detected in its structure. Not less unreasonable is it to deny the inspiration of such a book as the Bible, because one sacred writer says that on a given occasion twenty-four thousand, and another says that twenty-three thousand, men were slain. Surely a Christian may be allowed to tread such objections under his feet.[14]

For various reasons, including the heightened consciousness of language and meaning in twentieth-century philosophy, Christian theologians today are not quite so casual about the question of errors in the Bible. After all, it would be hard to maintain both that the Bible is true and that it contains errors. That there seem to be discrepancies like the one Hodge pointed to cannot be denied. But what conclusions are we to draw from the existence of apparent discrepancies?

It seems to me that the proper thing to do is to draw virtually no conclusions. We should remember that there have also been blemishes of another sort in the Bible, i.e. mistaken readings. Our best contemporary translations yield a different reading here and there than the King James Bible with which many generations of English-speaking Christians lived and died. If we are correct in assuming that our contemporary translations are based on older and purer Hebrew and Greek manuscripts, we must take it that our forefathers misread certain texts. This raises an interesting question: Was God able to speak to His people and bless them through His Word if that Word came to them by means of texts that were imperfect or "corrupt" (to use the theological term) in certain respects? The answer is clearly *yes*. We should then go on to ask whether God can also speak to His people by means of a Bible in which they seem to see discrepancies. Again the answer is yes. God's people can indeed be blessed through the reading of such a Bible—provided they do not jump to conclusions where no conclusions are warranted. One need not understand every passage in the Bible in order to be blessed and edified through Bible reading.

We should be especially careful not to read into the Bible meanings that simply are not there. This mistake has often been made with regard to the first chapters of Genesis: much of what theologians have asserted by way of exegesis or explanation of these chapters simply is not required by the text. We must learn to be more sober in our reading of Scripture and be willing to say that some disagreements about the meaning of specific passages do not now seem capable of resolution.

VI

To take such a sober and submissive attitude toward the Bible is to accept Scripture as the final authority in any dispute about the meaning of the Christian faith. The Westminster Confession (1646) affirms: "The Supreme Judge, by which all controversies of religion are to be determined, and all decrees of councils, opinions of ancient writers, doctrines of men, and private spirits, are to be examined, and in whose sentence we are to rest, can be no other but the Holy Spirit speaking in the Scripture."[15]

These words sound direct, final, almost harsh—and surely out of tune with our times. Any such submission to Scripture strikes modern man as a manifestation of an outdated authoritarian mentality. Hans Küng informs us that the Enlightenment "demythologized authority" and comments: ". . . no truth is accepted without being submitted to the judgment of reason, merely on the authority of the Bible or tradition or the Church, but only after a careful scrutiny."[16] We are reminded here of a famous accusation that Dietrich Bonhoeffer made against Karl Barth, namely, that Barth's theology of revelation is in effect a "positivism of revelation," a "like it or lump it" approach. Apparently a more critical attitude is called for.[17] We are also reminded of Lessing's complaint that the Protestant Bible is a "paper pope" claiming the same sort of arbitrary authority beyond appeal as the pope in Rome.[18]

VII

Such complaints, of course, are a far cry from the reverence and deep love for the Bible which we encounter in the Reformation era. The dictum *sola scriptura* (by Scripture alone) was not meant as burdensome but as a liberation from false authorities, traditions and doctrines that had long held Christian spirituality back. The attitude of submission to Scripture provided common ground for Christians to stand on—whether collectively or singly—in the face of false claims to their allegiance. The Enlightenment had not yet "demythologized authority."

The *sola scriptura* principle thus brought a measure of clarity to the theological debates that raged in the early sixteenth century, for it required a continual return to the source. Peter Beyerhaus observes:

> The decisive question in Martin Luther's controversy with the papists was this. What must Christians in general, and more specifically teachers of the Church, regard as the source and measuring stick for their doctrinal statements? His opponents endeavored to refute him by arguments taken from the tradition of the fathers and councils. Luther held fast to the principle that Scripture alone was the normative foundation of all preaching and teaching within the Church. Thus the slogan "*sola scriptura*" became the bed rock of evangelical faith and action.[19]

To this statement should be added an emphasis we find especially in Calvin, namely, that the Holy Spirit's testimony in the heart of the believer means that there is divine guidance in Bible reading. For Calvin, the Word and the Spirit are linked. This is not to say that the believer may equate his own interpretation (especially when it differs from that of other believers) with the Word of God. A failure to be properly submissive may well lead to misinterpretation and misunderstanding. Human pride can twist the Bible's meaning.

In our pride we so often want to see the rationale, the justification or explanation, for what is believed. Calvin warns against speculating about what might lie behind God's will, for when we speculate we are forgetting that

> . . . it is very wicked merely to investigate the causes of God's will. For his will is, and rightly ought to be, the cause of all things that are . . . For God's will is so much the highest rule of righteousness that whatever he wills, by the very fact that he wills it, must be considered righteous. When, therefore, one asks why God has so done, we must reply: because he willed it. But if you proceed further to ask why he so willed, you are seeking something greater and higher than God's will, which cannot be found.[20]

What Calvin is telling us here is that when God reveals something to us, we must be satisfied to know *that* it is the case and must not insist on knowing *why* it is the case. which is also the point Lev Shestov makes in his attack on reason (see p. 46 above). Certain things remain mysterious for us. The presence of evil in this world is a mystery, but so is God's unfathomable saving grace!

Bible reading calls for a certain attitude, then. The phrase "faith seeking understanding," which stems from Anselm and serves nicely to sum up the attitude toward faith and reason taken by Augustine, can help us there. The Bible's message is grasped first of all in faith—a childlike faith and trust. It can also be understood to some extent, although some believers make more progress in this regard than others do. Still, understanding often comes slowly, and certain passages remain dark and obscure to us even today, despite the thousands of books that have been written to clarify the Bible's message. Sometimes God's people have to wait a long, long time before this or that aspect of His message to them becomes clear. This lesson is all too easily forgotten in our busy, impatient world.

CHAPTER SIX

HISTORY AND TRADITION

I

CHRISTIANS like to distinguish between "living" truth and "dead" truth, and they often warn that orthodoxy can become dead and cold if it is not animated by a warm faith and piety. Truth is not an inanimate object; it is like a living organism that needs to be nourished daily. The English poet John Milton had an organic notion of truth in mind when he declared that a man's truth can become his heresy:

> Truth is compared in Scripture to a streaming fountain; if her waters flow not in a perpetual progression, they sicken into a muddy pool of conformity and tradition. A man may be a heretic in the truth; and if he believes things only because his Pastor says so, or the Assembly so determines, without knowing other reason, though his belief be true, yet the very truth he holds becomes his heresy.[1]

The Enlightenment, in its own way, also worried about such dangers, and therefore proclaimed that each person must think and judge for himself. In his essay "What Is Enlightenment?" Immanuel Kant writes:

> Through laziness and cowardice a large part of mankind, even after nature has freed them from alien guidance, gladly remain immature. It is because of laziness and cowardice that it is so easy for others to usurp the role of guardians. It is so comfortable to be a minor! If I have a book which provides meaning for me, a pastor who has conscience for me, a doctor who will judge my diet for me and so on, then I do not need to exert myself. I do not have any need to think; if I can pay, others will take over the tedious job for me.[2]

We are not to rely on tradition or external authority; rather, we are to use our rational faculties and decide matters on our own. If we fail to do so, we "remain immature." Thus Kant informs us that "the motto of the enlightenment" is "Have the courage to use your own intelligence!"[3]

The Reformation parallels the Enlightenment in its distrust of tradition and its rejection of the notion that the common man needs someone above him to do his thinking for him. Yet the Reformation does not glorify reason or "intelligence" and make each individual his own supreme authority. The Reformation emphasis is rather that *the Bible* belongs to the people—to each and every believer. The individual has access to the source of truth and is able to keep his beliefs fresh and alive by constantly subjecting them to the judgment of God's Word, which is the supreme standard.

Some thinkers believe that Protestantism went too far in its reverence for the Bible. Hans Küng writes: "Just as some Catholics believe less in God and his Christ than in the Church . . . so do many Protestants believe *in* the Bible."[4] Donald Wells complains about the "Protestant thesis of bibliocracy," by which he means the belief that "the scriptures contained all that man needed to know."[5] Such a charge, if taken literally, is hardly just: the Reformation is well known for its emphasis on learning broadly conceived. It recognized that there is much more to be studied than just the Bible. What really lies behind such criticism of the Protestant mind is uneasiness about the thesis that Scripture enjoys an exclusive authority. Shouldn't its authority be tempered by history or tradition?

In a book entitled *The Spirit of Protestantism,* Robert McAfee Brown describes the question of authority as the "Achilles' heel of Protestantism."[6] All too often, the Protestant rejection of the church's authority to interpret the Bible has led to subjectivism: each believer decided for himself what God's message meant. This may not have been the intention of the Reformers, but various scholars view it as the actual outcome of their work. Richard Popkin writes: "The Pandora's box that Luther opened at Leipzig [by questioning the church's authority] was to have the most far-reaching consequences, not just in theology but throughout man's entire intellectual realm."[7]

II

In their search for common ground to settle disputes about the meaning of the Christian faith and its doctrines, the Reformers turned to the Bible. But can such disputes *always* be settled by appealing to the Bible? It is far from obvious that they can. F. F. Bruce therefore observes: "The possession of a common Bible does not guarantee religious unity: very much depends on the way in which this common Bible is read and understood."[8] The Reformation wanted to shake off certain patterns that had developed in Bible reading, but it was not able to obliterate the past altogether. Because we are historical beings, we cannot help but be influenced by the past in one way or another in our Bible reading, nor should we even make this our aim. James Orr writes:

> We are more dependent on the past than we think even in our interpretation of Scripture; and it would be as futile for any man to attempt to draw his system of doctrine at first hand from Scripture, as it would be for a man of science to draw his scientific knowledge direct from nature, unaided by text-books, or the laborious researches of the myriad workers in the same field.[9]

What Orr is getting at is nicely illustrated by the story of Philip and the Ethiopian eunuch who was reading a passage in the prophecy of Isaiah as he traveled home from Jerusalem. This man came to Scripture with virtually no background to help him understand, and so Philip had to ask him: "Do you understand what you are reading?" When the answer was no, Philip gave him background knowledge to make the passage comprehensible: ". . . beginning with this scripture he told him the good news of Jesus" (see Acts 8:26ff).

Scripture as a whole is comprehensible, but to gain a knowledge of Scripture as a whole takes time. In other words, we need experience in Bible reading. Moreover, the acts in which God reveals Himself call for commentary and explanation, for their meaning is sometimes far from obvious. James I. Packer tells us that ". . . the biblical position is that the mighty acts of God are not revelation to man at all, except in so far as they are accompanied by words of God to explain them. Leave man to guess God's mind and purpose, and he will guess wrong; he can know it only by being told it."[10]

III

Protestantism has left itself open to criticism in that some Protestants have seemed to work with Scripture in an arbitrary, subjective manner. Naturally, this has elicited comments from Catholic quarters. Luther was asked repeatedly how he could be so sure he was right if this meant that a great many popes and bishops and learned men of the church were wrong. Wouldn't it be wiser to take numbers and consensus and the views of earlier generations into account a bit more? Shouldn't Protestantism stay away from any a-historical "fundamentalism" that does not allow history to play a major role in Biblical interpretation?

The Catholic apologist G. K. Chesterton presents a defense of tradition in which he asks us to respect the opinions of our forbears. Cleverly he points out that there is something democratic about this: tradition is ". . . democracy extended through time. It is trusting to a consensus of human voices rather than to some isolated or arbitrary record." Many of the great men are no longer with us, but this does not mean that we should disregard their opinions, according to Chesterton:

> Tradition may be defined as an extension of the franchise. Tradition means giving votes to the most obscure of all classes, our ancestors. It is the democracy of the dead. Tradition refuses to submit to the small and arrogant oligarchy of those who merely happen to be walking about. All democrats object to men being disqualified by the accident of birth; tradition objects to their being disqualified by the accident of death. Democracy tells us not to neglect a good man's opinion, even if he is our groom; tradition asks us not to neglect a good man's opinion, even if he is our father.[11]

IV

In contemporary theology there is a keen awareness of the need for an interpretive context in Bible reading. History, in the sense of the collective experience of a society or a well-defined group, is often appealed to as the context. The Bible is then read not in a social-historical vacuum but with an eye to a particular situation and particular needs.

Under the influence of the sociology of knowledge, theologians have begun to propose "theologies" that arise from the situations of the various identifiable groups that make up the world's population. "Black theology," for example, is then the product of the interaction between the Bible and the historical experience of blacks. In the process, black self-awareness and needs become normative. In a book on "black theology," James Cone claims that the common experience of black people is "the supreme test of truth." He explains:

> Concretely, this means that Black Theology is not prepared to accept any doctrine of God, man, Christ, or Scripture which contradicts the black demand for freedom now. It believes that any religious idea which exalts black dignity and creates a restless drive for freedom must be affirmed.
>
> When the question is asked, "On what authority, in the last resort, do we base our claim that this or that doctrine is part of the Gospel and therefore true?" Black Theology must say: "If the doctrine is compatible with or enhances the drive for black freedom, then it is the gospel of Jesus Christ. If the doctrine is against or indifferent to the essence of blackness as expressed in Black Power, then it is the work of the Antichrist." It is as simple as that.[12]

Albert J. Cleage, Jr. expresses the same point emphatically: "For the black man everything must be judged in terms of Black liberation. There is but one authority, and that is the Black experience."[13]

Feminist theology takes a similar approach in its commitment to the liberation theme. Margaret Maxey calls for an "instrumental theology" which would "have the task of liberating women from past models." Theology can contribute to liberation by "authorizing models for self-expression through more plausible life-styles and social institutions." Once again historical experience becomes normative. Maxey writes: "Once we recognize that the process of liberation is an *authorizing process*—one displacing the 'authority' of past dominant models-for-self-understanding and behavior by constructing more meaningful or authoritative models—then theology might once again perform its central humanizing task."[14]

V

These examples show us that the notion of a historical context for reading Scripture can be misused. But they should not lead us to disregard history as we read Scripture. It simply is not possible for us to look at the Bible as though all the centuries that separate us from the Bible writers contained no history. We should not even wish for such a reading of Scripture.

The interaction between history and the Bible can be fruitful. God's special revelation was not meant to be self-contained: it was intended to light up history and the world for us. God's Word is a "lamp to my feet and a light to my path" (Psalm 119:105). When we use a lamp, we do not stare into its glare but use the light it gives us to get a better look at the world around us. And so it is with the Bible. We use it best and learn to fathom its meaning when we bear in mind that it is our guide for life in this world. It should never be our aim to isolate the Bible from history and the world we live in.

Because mainline Protestantism has always realized this (even though there have indeed been Protestants who tried to read the Bible "in isolation"), it has promoted genuine Christian scholarship, that is, not just scholarship undertaken by people who happen to be Christians but scholarship in the light of the Bible. The guidance of God's Word is essential for gaining a proper understanding of history and nature, and a knowledge of history and nature in turn enriches our comprehension of the Bible. Great gains in Biblical scholarship have been made in our century because of what archeologists, for example, have discovered. Thus we should reject any suggestion that the Protestant emphasis on the Bible as the supreme authority is intended to draw the Christian's attention away from history, nature and the world we live in.

VI

The interpretive context that seems to be needed for the reading of Scripture can also be called *tradition.* Many Protestants are hesitant to use the word *tradition* because they associate it with a Roman Catholic tendency to diminish Scripture's authority by subordinating it to the church as the authorized interpreter. Gradually this reluctance is being overcome, and there is now talk to the effect that Catholics and Protestants may be closer together on the relation between Scripture and tradition than many people have realized.

If there is indeed a *rapprochement* possible, the key to it is the recognition that Scripture itself is in some significant sense tradition. Various parts of the Bible seem to have existed in oral form before they were written down, and thus they were handed on from generation to generation as tradition or "Überlieferung." Included in such tradition was not just what God had done but also the meaning of His saving acts as He Himself had revealed it.

The apostolic teaching is also tradition in such a sense. *Tradition* is a Latin term, and behind it is the idea of "handing over." Think here of the Letter of Jude, in which we find an appeal "to contend for the faith which was once for all delivered to the saints" (vs. 3). The legacy or tradition that has been given us must be defended and passed on to the next generation! It was in this spirit that Paul wrote about the institution of the Lord's supper: "For I received from the Lord what I also delivered to you, that the Lord Jesus on the night when he was betrayed took bread . . ." (I Corinthians 11:23).

Scripture can also function as tradition in the sense that it is a large book whose many parts and passages shed light on one another. Therefore the Reformers emphasized that Scripture is its own interpreter (*sacra scriptura sui ipsius interpres*). The darker, more obscure passages are to be read in the light of the clearer passages. This is not to say that archeological findings may not also be used to shed light on Scripture's meaning; the point is simply that Scripture itself enjoys the primacy or priority in this regard, and that its resources as its own interpreter are greater than is often realized.

This should be borne in mind especially when we interpret what the Bible says about Jesus. The New Testament narratives about Him need to be read in the light of the Old Testament promises and prophecies. Jesus Himself illustrated this when He walked with the two men of Emmaus and interpreted for them the meaning of the crucifixion, which had dashed their hopes: "And beginning with Moses and all the prophets, he interpreted to them in all the scriptures the things concerning himself" (Luke 24:27).

It needs to be emphasized especially that the Old Testament is indispensable as tradition and interpretive context for understanding the New. Much theological harm has resulted from the neglect of the Old Testament: alien interpretive contexts and schemes have been introduced to bring out the meaning of the New Testament.[15] Rudolf Bultmann, for example, looked to contemporary philosophy to unlock the meaning of the New Testament, whose message, he argued, had to be "demythologized." And it is significant that when efforts were made to absorb Christianity into the Gnostic movement, the Old Testament was perceived as a barrier. The Old Testament tradition serves to keep New Testament interpretation on track.

VII

This conception of Scripture as a type of tradition should be borne in mind when the Protestant principle of *sola scriptura* (by Scripture alone) is discussed. Robert McAfee Brown observes that ". . . Protestants do not rely on *sola Scriptura* in quite the pure way that Reformation Sunday sermons would suggest."[16] The *sola scriptura* emphasis has been both a strength and a weakness, according to Brown. It has sometimes led to efforts to read the Bible "in isolation," ignoring history and nature. A "faulty assumption" was made, namely, that ". . . it is possible to 'leapfrog,' as it were, over 1900 years of Christian history, and read the Bible as though nothing had happened since the documents themselves were composed."[17]

Undoubtedly various Protestants have been guilty of "leapfrogging," but the Reformers themselves certainly did not mean to suggest that the Bible could be read in such a manner. Bernard Ramm argues: "The *sola scriptura* of the Reformers did not mean a total rejection of tradition. It meant only that Scripture had the final word on a subject. The use by the Reformers of the writings of the Fathers shows how deeply they were nourished by Christian tradition."[18]

VIII

The line between Catholicism and Protestantism was clear in the Reformation era, especially when the Council of Trent (1545-63) definitively repudiated the Protestant conception of Scripture by declaring tradition and Scripture equal sources of the faith. In our time there seems to be some convergence underway between the two sides, but one great barrier remains—papal infallibility. According to this doctrine, when the pope speaks *ex cathedra* (i.e. in a strictly defined official capacity), he is infallible. It should be noted that infallibility is not claimed for the papal encyclicals, some of which have proven rather controversial.

The doctrine of papal infallibility, which was not proclaimed until 1870, can be viewed as a magnification of certain elements in the Catholic understanding of tradition, elements which Protestants find objectionable. Since many Protestant churches have adopted creeds, the notion of the church as possessing some sort of teaching authority is not altogether foreign. But the suggestion that the church or its leader possesses infallibility will not win acceptance among Protestants. Papal infallibility remains a barrier to closer fellowship between Protestants and Catholics, even though the popes have been very sparing in the use of this power.

Papal infallibility has also been a vexation to some contemporary Catholic theologians, e.g. Hans Küng, who wishes to ascribe infallibility (in the sense of "indeceivability" or "indefectibility" in the truth) to the *church* instead.[19] Küng's position, however, has not won official endorsement but has rather been condemned.

The doctrine of papal infallibility raises the interesting question whether a pope could be a heretic. Various popes were seriously delinquent in morals; could a pope also stray in doctrine? One of the teachings of Honorius I, who was pope from 625 to 638, was repudiated forty-two years after his death at the Council of Constantinople, and Honorius himself was condemned as a "favorer of heretics." In the Middle Ages it was generally assumed that a pope could indeed become a heretic, which would have the effect of disqualifying him as head of the church. But in the Middle Ages the doctrine of papal infallibility was not yet in effect. It is hard to see how any pope in our time, now officially infallible, could be a heretic if he chose to invoke his power of infallibility to justify his deviant doctrine.

IX

The doctrine of papal infallibility can serve as a reminder that a proper respect for tradition as helpful for reading Scripture should not lead us to forget that we must distinguish between good and bad tradition. In other words, tradition can be mistaken. But if we are ever to pronounce it mistaken, we must have some yardstick or criterion.

That yardstick, of course, is Scripture. H. J. McSorley writes: ". . . Scripture can be regarded as a 'norma normans, non normata' for the faith of the church and for the official dogmatic norms articulated by the church. This means that dogmas 'always have to be measured against Scripture.' "[20] Scripture, in other words, is the unnormed norm; it is the norm for the development of tradition in a healthy sense, for it is itself subject to no norm.

One way to express what it means that Scripture is the norm is to think of it as our interpretive anchor. Tradition operating on its own represents a series of interpretations, which in turn need to be interpreted, until we wind up with interpretations of interpretations of interpretations. The result of all this interpretation is that we drift ever farther away from our moorings, just as a story retold by person after person tends to change. But if Scripture is the ultimate norm for tradition, it can serve as an anchor. We do not escape the necessity of interpretation, but we keep interpreting the same source, i.e. the purest text of Scripture. This insistence on retaining the source is part of what is meant by the *sola scriptura* principle.

In this notion of Scripture as interpretive anchor or unnormed norm we have the basis for a positive attitude toward experience and history (i.e. tradition) as a secondary authority for Christians. To simply take human history and experience as such to be normative would be to fall prey to historicism (see p. 34 above). However, to recognize that the development of Christian life in obedience to God's Word represents "normed history" is to allow that there can be tradition or a body of shared experience and insights and understanding that can serve to hold Christians together, can help settle disputes about the meaning of the faith, and can give us a great deal of guidance in daily life. The wisdom and insight that comes to expression in the Bible's "wisdom literature" (e.g. the book of Proverbs) represents tradition in this healthy sense: "Hear, my son, your father's instruction, and reject not your mother's teaching" (Proverbs 1:8). The verse before gives us the key to such "traditional" wisdom: "The fear of the Lord is the beginning of knowledge."

We see, then, that the appeal to history and past experience ("We have always believed that" or "We have always done it this way") should not be ruled out altogether as illegitimate. The point to remember is that Scripture comes first; history or tradition or experience is subordinate to it, not coordinate with it. Tradition may help believers grasp the meaning of Scripture, but it can never be allowed to contradict Scripture. If it does clash with Scripture, we have tradition in the unhealthy, harmful sense, the kind of tradition against which the Reformers rebelled.

X

This conception of tradition can also help clarify the place and function of theology and of Christian thought generally. Theologizing is an ongoing process; that is to say, it is historical in character. A few theologians may prize innovativeness and uniqueness as the supreme value, but most freely admit that they stand in a tradition. Thus there is a Calvinist theological tradition, a Lutheran tradition, and so forth.

Theology—or the work of our best theologians—deserves respect and consideration when differences are discussed among Christians. Theology does not represent common ground in the sense that all Christians can or should take it as their starting point, but the best theology is potentially helpful and should be regarded as part of tradition in the healthy sense. Anthony Thiselton suggests that ". . . systematic theology might be said to represent the end-process, to date, of the process of tradition in which the Christian community seeks to arrive at an understanding of the biblical text."[21]

But the possibility of bad or unhealthy tradition also arises here. Just as Jesus condemned the thoroughly mistaken tradition of the Pharisees (see Mark 7:1-13), it might prove necessary to reject a theological tradition as contrary to the central thrust of the gospel and therefore an *obstacle* to the understanding of the Biblical message. This is essentially what the Reformers did. We must be historically aware also in that we realize that theological work undertaken on the wrong foundation will not be of value for the interpretation of Scripture. A bad tree does not bear good fruit, Jesus reminds us (Luke 6:43). If we want good fruit, we must pluck it from a good tree, and if we want theological guidance that will enable us to deepen our understanding of Scripture, we must read theologians who build on the proper foundation.

PART THREE

HERESY AND ORTHODOXY

IT is the task of the church—not of Christians acting on their own—to define the Christian faith. The church has undertaken this assignment from time to time in history when the purity of the faith was threatened by ways of thinking incompatible with the gospel. The ultimate criterion or standard is Scripture as God's special revelation, but Scripture is to be read against the background of history, experience and nature. Interpretation is inevitable, and therefore tradition can play a positive role, provided it is not elevated above Scripture.

To admit these points is to allow the concepts of heresy and orthodoxy a place in contemporary Christian thinking. Yet there are people today who regard the widespread commitment to "pluralism" as leaving no room for these two related concepts (Chapter 7). Another problem that should be faced is that the concept of orthodoxy might be understood as requiring near-total agreement on the theological level (Chapter 8). If heresy is to be defined in a manner that still allows for legitimate disagreement between Christian theologians, it will have to be in a way that stresses spiritual motives and factors (Chapter 9). Finally, certain implications with regard to confessional unity remain to be drawn, especially in relation to the question of orthodoxy and "orthopraxis" (Chapter 10).

CHAPTER SEVEN

PLURALISM AND DIVERSITY

I

THE term *pluralism* is widely embraced today as a way to resolve potentially nasty disputes. When there are differences between people, we are told that this need not cause a problem, for we live in a pluralistic society. We rejoice in our diversity. Yet a nagging question remains: Are there limits? At what point does pluralism become fragmentation, chaos, sheer relativism, or even nihilism?

Many theologians are enthusiastic about pluralism, but there are also concerns raised. George Lindbeck suggests that pluralism may prove to be "unmanageable." In the "dangerous pluralism of contemporary theology," it turns out that ". . . the practitioners of different methods are often not able even meaningfully to disagree."[1] A breakdown in communication is possible.

Pluralism in theology is hard to separate from subjectivism and relativism. James I. Packer warns against "theological agnosticism," by which he means a renunciation of truth as traditionally understood: ". . . we are not entitled to infer from the fact that a group of people are drawing nearer to each other that any of them is drawing nearer to the truth."[2]

We saw earlier that our tension-filled world is made uneasy by the thought of conflict. People today want to see conflicts de-fused (which is not the same as resolved) and therefore quickly turn to the rhetoric of tolerance. Tolerance, of course, can be justified in various different ways; the justification we tend to offer today, however, is in effect a gentle relativism which is often expressed in the language of pluralism. Such a relativism leaves no room for the concepts of heresy and orthodoxy but instead takes an eclectic approach to truth. In a study of the Enlightenment, a formative period of Western history to which our contemporary conception of tolerance owes a great deal, Peter Gay writes:

> Relativism, Eclecticism, and toleration are so intimately related that they cannot be strictly separated even in thought. Relativism is a way of looking at the world, the recognition that no single set of convictions has absolute validity; Eclecticism is the philosophical method consequent on relativism—since no system has the whole truth, and most systems have some truth, discriminating selection among systems is the only valid procedure. Toleration, finally, is the political counterpart of this world view and this method: it is a policy for a large and varied society.[3]

II

This is not to say, however, that *pluralism* simply means relativism. The term actually has a variety of meanings—in fact, too many. It is one of the overworked words of our time. Some years ago Philip Wogaman warned: "The term 'pluralism' has, in fact, been invoked so routinely in current discussion as to risk becoming a mere cliché."[4]

For various writers the term does have a central core of meaning, which is aptly summarized by George Forell as "the existence of various and contradictory approaches to life simultaneously, which can neither be uprooted nor overcome, absorbed or ignored."[5] Forell confesses that he regards such pluralism as threatening. For many people today, on the other hand, it is a part of the modern outlook to be cherished, and a great improvement on the closed-mindedness of earlier ages. Will Herberg observes:

> In America religious pluralism is thus not merely a historical and political fact; it is, in the mind of the American, the primordial condition of things, an essential aspect of the American Way of Life, and therefore in itself an aspect of religious belief. Americans, in other words, believe that the plurality of religious groups is a proper and legitimate condition. However much he may be attached to his own church, however dimly he may regard the beliefs and practices of other churches, the American tends to feel rather strongly that total religious uniformity, even with his own church benefiting thereby, would be something undesirable and wrong, indeed scarcely conceivable. Pluralism of religions and churches is something quite axiomatic to the American.[6]

Is pluralism compatible with monotheistic religion? It would appear that it is, for many adherents of such monotheistic faiths as Christianity and Judaism have embraced it. But there are thinkers who sense a tension between pluralism and the commitment to abide by the word and authority of a single god. Thus the pluralist trend (which, taken literally, is a celebration of "manyness") is leading to talk of a revival of polytheism (belief in many gods). David L. Miller, in a book entitled *The New Polytheism: Rebirth of the Gods and Goddesses,* writes: "Our culture is *apparently* pluralistic; *actually* it is polytheistic." In monotheistic thinking there lurks the danger of "social and psychological fascism." Miller urges us to reflect on the theological implications and presuppositions of our pluralistic society: "There is an implicit polytheism always lurking in democracy." His book calls us to a recognition: ". . . insofar as our diverse pluralistic ways of thought are grounded in some deep concern (which is what the Gods name), the thinking is not only pluralistic but is also polytheistic."[7]

III

The term *pluralism* has a significant meaning in relation to society and politics: it represents an alternative to collectivism and individualism as major social philosophies.[8] Collectivism tends to absorb the various institutions and organizations that make up society into some dominant institution, such as the totalitarian state in the twentieth century or the church in the Middle Ages. Individualism, on the other hand, recognizes mainly separate human beings as components of society and awards them various rights vis-à-vis the state, but it does not take proper account of the status and rights of other entities such as families and free associations.

Abraham Kuyper and Herman Dooyeweerd, two Calvinist thinkers, have developed a conception of society as made up of various sovereign "spheres" that are not to interfere with one another or attempt to exercise jurisdiction over each other, e.g. family, school, church, business enterprise. This vision of society, which is often referred to as the "sphere sovereignty" view, has also come to be called pluralism since it rejects both individualism and the collectivist, implicitly totalitarian notion that all such "spheres" are parts or branches of one organization—the all-powerful state. Because this conception of pluralism is not the same as the one identified earlier by Forell, it should be further qualified with an adjective: perhaps it could be called structural or societal pluralism.[9]

This societal pluralism is rooted—in Dooyeweerd's case, at least—in an ontological pluralism, that is, a conception of reality that distinguishes a plurality of irreducibly different types of being and functioning. Materialism would be an example of a *monistic* ontology: everything is matter. There are also ontologies that we would call *dualistic* since they proclaim that whatever exists is either matter or mind. In a *pluralistic* ontology more categories are distinguished. Thus Dooyeweerd's societal pluralism presupposes an ontological pluralism. In other words, he regards the differences between the church and the family, for example, as ultimately ontological in character.

When Christians speak up in favor of "pluralism," they often have this societal pluralism in mind, a pluralism that resists encroachment by the state on the church, the school, the family, and the business enterprise. Even if they do not use the terminology of Kuyper and Dooyeweerd, they are well aware that God has created the family with an integrity of its own such that it must not be swallowed up by the state, which is what tends to happen in totalitarian countries.

IV

Another meaning given to the term *pluralism* is the recognition and acceptance of racial, ethnic and cultural diversity. It cannot be denied that there is a plurality of languages, races and cultures present on this earth. Various thinkers insist on using the term plural*ism* to refer to this state of affairs.

The recognition of the significance of cultural and ethnic plurality or diversity goes back a long way in history. The term *pluralism* as used in this chapter is a comparatively recent one, but there were earlier terms that stood for the same set of issues, such as *historicism*. In a recent book dealing with historical consciousness we read: "The crisis of historicism has become the crisis of pluralism."[10]

All through recorded history mankind has lived with ethnic and cultural diversity. Thus there have long been groups of people speaking different languages. But for most of human history there was very little *awareness* of this state of affairs and its potential significance. With the heightening of historical consciousness in Europe since the eighteenth century, Western man found himself faced with the set of questions usually referred to as the "problem of historicism."

The linguistic diversity was indeed amazing, but it did not seem threatening. After all, there is nothing exclusive about language. An individual of reasonable intelligence is capable of learning a number of languages and of expressing himself reasonably well in several. But what about religions? If a human being can be multilingual, can he also be multi-religious? And can a person embrace more than one set of values at the same time? Hendrik Kraemer points to the problem we face here: "It is the great and painful privilege of our period of history that the plurality of religions and normative standards of truth and value in fields other than religion proper presses itself upon us in an inescapable way."[11]

Language, culture, social organization, and religion can never be fully separated. Yet it seems that some sort of distinction is called for here. The diversity and plurality in linguistic and ethnic respects, at least, should be regarded in positive terms as an outcome of God's determination to create a variegated world. We reject the notion that any one race is superior *per se* to others, and we freely admit that the world's languages cannot be ranked in a manner that would allow us to determine with regard to any given pair of languages which one is superior. We accept ethnic and linguistic diversity and rejoice in it.

V

When it comes to religious diversity, an extra factor enters the picture—sin. Plurality or "pluralism" in religious respects is not a reason for rejoicing, for it means that the original religious unity of mankind has been lost. The book of Genesis tells us about the formation of two religious communities after the fall into sin—one of belief and the other of unbelief. And since unbelief has nothing to hold it together, it has undergone further fragmentation in history. The great commission with which Christ charged His disciples (see Matthew 28:18-20) is in effect a mandate to overcome this religious "pluralism," to work toward its elimination.

I put the term *pluralism* in quotation marks in the paragraph above because I see no good reason for using a word with an "ism" ending to refer to this regrettable state of affairs. The plurality of religions or faith communities should *not* be regarded as a reflection of God's will for His creation. In this regard it does not parallel the ethnic and linguistic diversity discussed earlier, that is, the existence of a stunning array of languages and racial differences. Neither is it to be compared to societal pluralism, the recognition of family, church, school, and business enterprise as independent of one another and not subordinate to the state.

So-called "religious pluralism," of course, is intertwined with cultural variety and difference. That there is considerable cultural diversity in our world is not to be denied, but again I see no good reason for speaking of this diversity as "plural*ism*." To do so is to risk slipping into the gentle relativism which so many people embrace today as the rationale for tolerance.

Of course Christians have an understandable reason for being attracted to the language of pluralism and the gentle relativism it expresses. The gospel has stirred up opposition throughout human history, and Christians are still mocked and scorned today, especially in intellectual circles, where they are told repeatedly that well-educated people should know better than to believe a myth about a man rising from the dead. In such a climate Christians all too quickly look to pluralist rhetoric as a cheap and easy defense of their faith. Instead of bearing scorn and abuse silently or explaining what they believe in order to clear up the inevitable misconceptions, they allow their faith to be relativized. If all cultures and religions are equally good—this is essentially what the gentle relativism of our time comes to—then no one can reproach the Christian for his faith. Don't we live in a pluralistic society in which one person believes in Jesus Christ, a second in science and rationality, and a third in astrology?

VI

I am not suggesting that Christians should disregard religious differences or that they should practice the intolerance that has done so much harm to the Christian cause in the past. The question we need to face is whether Christians ought to embrace pluralism, which, as I indicated earlier, is a way of dealing with the question of tolerance. If the answer is no, that is, if the Christian is not to embrace pluralism in the sense of historicism and cultural relativism as his rationale for tolerance, how is he to approach this important issue of our time instead?

I believe the guidance needed is to be found in Scripture. The key passage on the question of the toleration of religious differences is the parable of the wheat and the tares, which we find recorded in Matthew 13:

> The kingdom of heaven may be compared to a man who sowed good seed in his field; but while men were sleeping, his enemy came and sowed weeds among the wheat, and went away. So when the plants came up and bore grain, then the weeds appeared also. And the servants of the householder came and said to him, "Sir, did you not sow good seed in your field? How then has it weeds?" He said to them, "An enemy has done this." The servants said to him, "Then do you want us to go and gather them?" But he said, "No; lest in gathering the weeds you root up the wheat along with them. Let both grow together until the harvest; and at harvest time I will tell the reapers, Gather the weeds first and bind them in bundles to be burned, but gather the wheat into my barn" (vs. 24-30).

Commentators on this passage like to point out that the weeds or tares are not easily distinguished from the wheat. And so it is with true and false teaching: false teaching often incorporates elements of the truth and therefore is not always distinguishable from the truth. Another factor, of course, is that the roots of the wheat and the tares are intertwined, which means that any attempt to uproot the tares would harm the wheat.

I believe we are to take this parable as a Biblical rationale for religious toleration. It must be admitted that its consequences were not always clearly recognized throughout the history of Christianity. Roland Bainton has pointed out various "expedients employed by persecutors to evade the liberal implications of the parable" and "devices for emasculating the parable."[12]

But in what respects and to what extent must Christians be tolerant? Political theorists have reminded us that there are limits to tolerance. And does a commitment to tolerance mean accommodating oneself to untruth? Stephen Neill, who speaks of "the painful issue of the intolerance of truth," asks: "How is the claim that one religion is true, or at least more true than another, to be reconciled with our principle of tolerance and of the plural society?"[13] J. Gresham Machen sounds a similar warning with regard to tolerance:

> There is a sense, of course, in which tolerance is a virtue. If by it you mean tolerance on the part of the state, the forbearance of majorities toward minorities, the resolute rejection of any measures of physical compulsion in propagating either what is true or what is false, then of course the Christian ought to favor tolerance with all his might and main, and ought to lament the widespread growth of intolerance in America to-day. Or if you mean by tolerance forbearance toward personal attacks upon yourself, or courtesy and patience and fairness in dealing with all errors of whatever kind, then again tolerance is a virtue. But to pray for tolerance apart from such qualifications, in particular to pray for tolerance without a careful definition of that of which you are to be tolerant, is just to pray for the breakdown of the Christian religion; for the Christian religion is intolerant to the core.[14]

The Reformers—including both Luther and Calvin—clearly went too far in the direction of intolerance because they did not sufficiently distinguish the role of the state from the role of the church. The question of tolerance needs to be raised separately for these two contexts. The seventeenth-century English philosopher John Locke recognized this point, and his views on tolerance have deeply affected Protestantism. Locke wrote: ". . . I esteem it above all things necessary to distinguish exactly the business of civil government from that of religion, and to settle the just bounds that lie between the one and the other." Locke did not by any means maintain that the church was obliged to tolerate teaching it regarded as false: the church ". . . has the power to remove any of its members who transgress the rules of its institution . . ."[15]

VII

Christians should not only tolerate religious and theological views that differ from their own; they should also be willing to discuss issues with people of opposing viewpoints in an effort to learn and to teach. Genuine openness in discussion is essentially a willingness to learn from one's discussion partner, although what one learns is not necessarily what one's partner *intends* to teach.

The same point can be made using the language of pluralism, but I have chosen to speak of tolerance instead. Still, it should be noted that various thinkers who do use the language of pluralism here are sober about the dangers and do not advocate relativism in the sense of a compliant willingness to forsake one's own position, as though one ought to enter the discussion without any position. Quite the contrary, for discussion in a "pluralistic" setting requires that each participant have a position and be able to presuppose a certain amount of agreement. David Tracy, who worries about a "mindless, chaotic pluralism of pure subjectivities," observes: "The heart of a responsible pluralism in any community of inquiry is to achieve enough basic consensus (especially on methodology and criteria) to allow critical discussion of both agreements and disagreements within the relevant community of inquiry."[16]

It should also be noted that "pluralism" is not always as tolerant as it appears. James Hitchcock warns against an "illusory pluralism" that may appear to promote tolerance but actually does the opposite. The appeal to "pluralism" is often a political gambit designed to get people to surrender positions to which they are deeply committed. An honest pluralism, according to Hitchcock, requires that people be self-conscious and forthright about their convictions: ". . . the real nature of pluralism . . . in a mass society can only mean the existence of a number of strong, cohesive, well-defined groups which work out a social relationship with one another through compromise but also through tension and a tenacious defense of their own interests and values."[17]

Serious differences cannot be ignored; we must learn to live with them. We will see next what this means for science and theology, where the differences and disagreements are of a theoretical nature.

CHAPTER EIGHT

THEORY AND DISAGREEMENT

I

DISAGREEMENT and conflict make people uneasy, for ours is an age of anxiety. One common response to conflict is to adopt the language of pluralism by proclaiming that disagreements don't really matter, just as it need not be a problem that some people have dark skin while others have light skin. People of different races are all beautiful in their own way, and so are different ideas.

Other people respond to conflict by declaring that the disagreements between people may be real (which involves admitting that some people, at least, are wrong) but are only theoretical and thus not important. The differences are literally academic in that they do not pose a practical problem or have any bearing on day-to-day affairs.

There are indeed such "academic" differences, but there are also differences of a different nature—political and economic differences. The differences between Stalin and Leon Trotsky that became painfully apparent after Lenin's death in 1924 had to do with political philosophy, but they were much more than academic. Trotsky was ruled a "heretic" and in 1927 was expelled from the Communist Party together with many of his followers. His dissent from Communist orthodoxy apparently cost him his life: he was assassinated in Mexico in 1940.

The philosopher Baruch Spinoza is another famous heretic who was literally excommunicated. The leaders of the synagogue in Amsterdam expelled him from the fellowship of the Jews in 1656 for his "evil opinions and works." Yet Lewis Feuer suggests that the issue was not so much theological deviance as power: excommunication ". . . was first and foremost a means by which the unity of the community, as conceived by its affluent leaders, was to be preserved. Excommunication could be used to bend the will of those intractable members who challenged the socio-economic power of the governing group."[1]

II

The concepts of heresy and orthodoxy do seem to function, then, in the political and economic sphere. They also play a role in the world of science and scholarship, where we would expect to find genuinely "academic" differences. It turns out that some of the differences in the scholarly world are more than academic. In various disciplines there is a reigning orthodoxy; dissenters or "heretics" have trouble getting teaching positions and research grants. Even philosophers, who should be the most flexible of all scholars in their thinking, can be distressingly narrow-minded about their discipline.

In the world of science and scholarship there is probably no better example of the concepts of orthodoxy and heresy at work than the psychoanalytic movement. Sigmund Freud, its founder, quickly attracted a number of followers and disciples, and among them were some men with ideas of their own—especially Carl Gustav Jung and Alfred Adler. In the literature on the disagreements that sprang up we find references to "heresy" and "apostasy."[2]

Freud himself led the way in the use of such language, describing Jung and Adler as "the two heretics."[3] His loyal follower and biographer Ernest Jones observes: "Jung often said he was by nature a heretic, which was why he was drawn at first to Freud's very heretical work."[4] Freud admitted that he had made a mistake in putting his trust in Jung, whom he later characterized as ". . . a person who was incapable of tolerating the authority of another, but who was still less capable of wielding it himself, and whose energies were ruthlessly devoted to the furtherance of his own interests."[5] Like many another battler for orthodoxy, Freud felt compelled to "contend for the faith." He complained:

> After exercising so much self-restraint in not coming to blows with opponents outside analysis, I now see myself compelled to take up arms against its former followers or people who still like to call themselves its followers . . . Anyone who has followed the growth of other scientific

movements will know that the same upheavals and dissensions commonly occur in them as well.[6]

III

The discipline most often associated with disagreement and strife is theology. And it is certainly true that there is plenty of variety—to use a less threatening term—among theologians. If theologians disagree often, can we safely brand their disagreements merely academic? Or is the life and health of the church at stake in every disagreement?

The important point to be made here is that theology as a science, a scholarly discipline, is to be distinguished from dogma. The locus of theology is the academic world, while dogma is part of the life of the church. Yet some theologians try to bring these two notions together. Gerhard Ebeling, for example, speaks of the "ecclesiastical character of theology." It is significant that he also thinks in terms of various "theologies" to be found in the New Testament.[7] If the gospel is itself a piece of theology, then the proclamation of the Word through the church can indeed be characterized as theology.

There are other theologians, however, who conceive of theology in narrower terms and carefully set it off from the dogmas of the church. James Orr distinguishes theology from both doctrine and dogma, describing it as "the reflective exercise of mind upon the doctrines of faith."[8] Herman Hoeksema likewise regards dogma as the province of the church rather than of theology: "A dogma may be defined as a doctrine elicited from Scripture, defined and officially established by the church."[9]

Dogmas function in the life of the church and help to structure and give substance to worship and liturgy. The creeds, in which the major dogmas are briefly stated, are not to be taken as pieces of theology; the Heidelberg Catechism, for example, speaks the down-to-earth, non-academic language of faith. Monika Hellwig explains the place of the creeds as follows: "The creeds used in worship are primarily a short form of profession of faith of the worshipping community; as such, they are not only a summary of the content of faith but also a prayer in which the believing community renews its commitment."[10]

The difference between creed and dogma, on the one hand,

and theology, on the other, becomes still clearer when we note that theology concerns itself in great detail with all sorts of matters which creeds and dogmas hardly touch. Dogmas are usually explicit in what they rule out, as one can see from reading the Athanasian Creed (see pp. 32-3 above), but they leave a certain amount of latitude within. The Christian creeds clearly affirm that God is the Creator, but they do not exegete the first chapter of Genesis for us. Herman Bavinck observes that ". . . it is remarkable that not a single confession says anything about the hexaemeron [the six days of creation] . . ."[11] Theologians have certainly pursued this matter and come up with all sorts of exegetical suggestions, but the church has not made up its mind and issued a dogmatic ruling.

IV

If theology is not dogma or doctrine, what is it? Etymologically it would appear to be the study of God or the science of God, and this is indeed how some traditional theologians have understood it. But the question quickly arises whether we know God as He is in Himself, as opposed to knowing Him in His relation to us, that is, by means of His revelation through which He bends down and accommodates Himself in order to make it possible for us to have knowledge of Him. If it is the latter, theology must somehow deal with the relation between God and the world He has made.

A representative definition of theology is offered by F. G. Healey: ". . . Christian theology may be described as systematic study of beliefs, practices and institutions which articulate Christian faith." Healey is careful not to suggest that Christian theology is simply the study of Christian faith.[12]

There is a good deal to be said for such a definition. It is fairly broad and takes in most of what is ordinarily understood by theology. At the same time it does not focus excessively on human subjectivity: theology, for Healey, is not the study of faith. Still, this definition is lacking in that it does not place enough emphasis on the normative dimension. Theology does not study God in any direct, unmediated way, but it certainly does concern itself with His revelation. Every science, ultimately, is judged and normed by revelation, but theology makes revelation its object.

Revelation is not studied in the abstract but as it impinges upon the lives of people who accept it or reject it. Hence we could better characterize theology as scholarly reflection on the appropriation of divine revelation by God's people in history. Such a definition preserves the central concern with the text of Scripture and its interpretation, while leaving room for historical theology (or church history) and systematic theology, which can never be divorced from the study of the development of dogma and doctrine. There is also room for the branches of theology that deal with the church and its functions, and on the periphery we could include a theology of the other religions, which would then be interpreted theologically as distorted and corrupt responses to God's pure revelation. The other religions are not to be understood in terms of themselves, for they are also subject to the normativity of revelation.

V

Theology understood by way of this definition should not simply be equated with what goes on in a theological seminary. The average seminary is in the business of training pastors and preachers—not theologians. Theological instruction does make up a good part of the curriculum for training preachers, but there are also courses in other areas, such as Hebrew grammar. A course in Hebrew grammar, when offered in a seminary, does not suddenly become theology, any more than courses in psychology, philosophy or public speaking should be branded theology simply because they are offered in a seminary.

On the other hand, it should be emphasized that theology and the theologian exist to serve the church, the people of God, just as science and scholarship are supposed to serve life. In a secondary sense, then, we may speak of theology as having an ecclesiastical bearing. Theological awareness and excitement should spur pastors on to preach. Therefore it is sometimes said that good theology should be preachable.

A note of caution is in order here, however. What a pastor preaches is not theology *per se*—or it should not be. A sermon is not an academic lecture but a proclamation of God's Word of grace and judgment. Proclamation is direct and bold, but not always nuanced and detailed. To a considerable extent, the application of the Biblical message must be left to God's people, that is, to those to whom the message is addressed. In this regard preaching resembles creeds and dogmas more than it does theology. Many pastors preach on the various articles that make up the Apostles' Creed or on the questions and answers of the Heidelberg Catechism. They do not—or should not—preach on a succession of topics drawn from a theological handbook.

Preaching, then, is less detailed and specific than theology. The theologian tries to fill in the blanks, as it were; he speaks where the creeds are silent. But for that very reason he must be tentative in what he offers. His ideas and solutions to doctrinal problems are intended to stimulate the thinking of other theologians (both lay and professional) and to help preachers better understand the meaning and message of God's Word. If there is real theological progress, part of a theologian's work may even be taken up into a doctrinal or dogmatic pronouncement by the church.

But the theologian does not operate in a vacuum. His ultimate criterion for the ideas he advances is Scripture itself. Just as God's people were instructed to check prophecy against prophecy to make sure they were not taken in by a false prophet or teacher,[13] the theologian compares his ideas with both the letter and spirit of Scripture. He is free to use his imagination and explore fresh possibilities, but he is not free to defend ideas which he knows to be contrary to Scripture.

VI

An important element in the definition of theology offered above is that the appropriation of divine revelation by God's people takes place *in history*. Theology is in no sense timeless. But what, exactly, does this mean? For Hans Küng it means that there are theological ideas which we can "no longer accept."[14] He writes: "The medieval world picture must be abandoned and the modern world picture consequently adopted, the result of which for theology itself will undoubtedly be the definitive transition to a new paradigm."[15]

Küng is correct in maintaining that a different outlook or worldview has supplanted the medieval conception of life. But is the mind of our time one and unified? The historian Crane Brinton writes: "The main theme of Western intellectual and moral history since about 1700 has been the *coexistence and mutual in-*

terpenetration of two very different world views, the Christian and that of the Enlightenment."[16]

There is more than one outlook or worldview competing for our allegiance, then. Hence we should not think in terms of a monolithic modern mind that simply rules out certain doctrines affirmed in the past as impossible to believe in our time. We face a choice. And as we make our choice we should remember that the worldview or outlook of an earlier age might well contain more truth than an "up-to-date" outlook clamoring for attention and acceptance. Even if we don't agree with all aspects of Martin Luther's conception of life in this world, we must admit that it contains a great deal of truth that is missing in the secular outlook that excludes the notions of human sinfulness and divine grace.

The understanding of life and the world prevalent in contemporary society differs in many ways from the outlook in Bible times. Thinkers who deal with hermeneutics or interpretation theory sometimes try to bridge the gap by making use of H. G. Gadamer's notion of the "two horizons." When we study the Bible or an ancient text, the two outlooks or worldviews (that of the text and that of the interpreter) must be brought together or fused in an act of understanding.[17] There must be a meeting of minds, as it were, between the Bible and modern man. Yet the two do not meet on equal terms, for the Bible enjoys normative status as God's revelation. The question for modern man is not what his modern outlook allows him to learn or accept from the Bible but to what extent his modern outlook conforms to the Bible's demands. Can one absorb modernity—in the sense of accepting the main lines of the Enlightenment's influence on our culture—and still be in line with the Bible? Are we to fuse the Enlightenment or modern outlook with the mind of the Bible?

Some theologians are inclined to try to get back behind the Enlightenment by essentially ignoring it and glorifying writers and thinkers who lived before it. To do this, however, is to ignore the historical dimension in theological thought. In its reflection theology must explore the way in which the Western church today, living under the impact of the Enlightenment, responds to God's revelation. Thus the Enlightenment inevitably comes within theology's purview.

Insofar as the theologian is supposed to help the church abide in orthodox doctrine, he must strive for what Thomas Oden calls "postmodern orthodoxy."[18] Oden complains about "Christian amnesia," which renders people unable to see beyond the bounds of modernity, the outlook from which Christians must free themselves by relearning their heritage. He writes that we must "correct the myopia of modernity" and strive for a "larger historical consciousness." What does he mean by "modernity"?

> By *modernity* I mean the overarching ideology of the modern period, characterized as it is by autonomous individualism, secularization, naturalistic reductionism, and narcissistic hedonism, which assumes that recent modes of knowing the truth are vastly superior to all older ways—a view that has recently presided over the precipitous deterioration of social structures and processes in the third quarter of the twentieth century. My aim is to help free persons from feeling intimidated by modernity, which, while it often seems awesome, is rapidly losing its moral power, and to grasp the emerging vision of a postmodern Christian orthodoxy.[19]

If theology is to work toward a "postmodern orthodoxy," it will have to address itself to a number of new tasks, two of which I will mention here. First, Crane Brinton talks about the "mutual interpenetration" of Christianity and the Enlightenment outlook. Theologians and Christians generally will have to ask themselves whether the overall thrust of the Enlightenment's conception of life is compatible with the Biblical outlook.

Second, traditional orthodox theology has been somewhat philosophically and epistemologically naive. A postmodern Christian orthodoxy will have to take careful account of the epistemological work of significant modern philosophers, especially Kant, Hegel and Husserl. A new statement is needed on the question of the limits of knowledge. More refined formulations should be possible in which various neglected modes and dimensions of knowing are dealt with. Much orthodox Christian theology is still tied to an essentially empiricistic and positivistic conception of knowledge and theoretical thought.

VII

To recognize the important historical dimension in theology is at the same time to set aside an ancient misconception, namely, that theology leaves no room for innovation or anything new. Princeton Seminary developed its own brand of Calvinism in the nineteenth century, but its theologians insisted that nothing was being taught at Princeton that had not also been taught elsewhere as part of Christian orthodoxy. When the Seminary was one hundred years old, Francis L. Patton, its president, proclaimed: "There has been a New Haven theology and an Andover theology; but there has never been a distinctively Princeton theology. Princeton's boast . . . is her unswerving fidelity to the theology of the Reformation."[20] Charles Hodge, who taught systematic theology at Princeton, likewise declared: "I am not afraid to say that a new idea has never originated in this Seminary."[21]

There is something commendable about this determination not to introduce anything new: the Princeton theologians were convinced that God's plan of salvation is fully and sufficiently revealed in Scripture. But at the same time their opposition to the idea of newness in theology was born of too narrow an understanding of theology, as we see when Hodge tells us that the Scriptures contain "all the facts of theology."[22] Scripture is central to theology, of course, but theology also deals with how the church has responded to Scripture and appropriated Scripture in its life over the centuries. Hodge's conception of theology is timeless; it excludes the historical dimension.

VIII

Theology, it must be emphasized again, is a scholarly discipline. Therefore it must leave room for disagreements of various sorts and remain tentative in its results, just as all science must be tentative. Abraham Kuyper observes:

> The hypotheses and dogmas of science can never be proved in the absolutely rigorous sense. And it can likewise be said that we do not know of a single natural scientific law which gives us irrevocable certainty. The most important principles from which science proceeds and on which it is based offer us no more than an approximate certainty . . .[23]

Theology is not by any means an exact science. Therefore a certain amount of imagination and speculation is needed; fresh approaches must be explored. Theodore W. Jennings, Jr. calls for "provisionality" in theology and argues for the "essential playfulness of theology."[24]

If such a view of theology is correct, we can take comfort in the thought that there is room for theoretical (or scholarly) disagreement in theology. In fact, disagreement and the clash of ideas can stimulate genuine progress and need not be taken as an indication that the theologians involved are drifting away from one another confessionally, although this possibility is not to be ruled out either. The point is simply that disagreement is a part of life in the world of science and scholarship.

Some theological diversity can be explained simply by the different materials theologians spend their time on. Because the book of Revelation is so full of Old Testament references and allusions, a theologian specializing in the Old Testament might read it differently than a theologian specializing in the New Testament and might see in it certain things that escaped the attention of his New Testament colleague. Such differences and disagreements are not a reason for worry; rather, they make theology an exciting discipline.

I am not saying there is no heresy among theologians; the point is rather that we should not start talking about heresy as soon as we encounter disagreement. Moreover, heresy is not essentially a theoretical or scholarly phenomenon, as we shall see in the next chapter. Heresy has something to do with unbelief and apostasy, with sin and willfulness.

CHAPTER NINE

HERESY AND APOSTASY

I

WE saw earlier that heresy is a much avoided topic, an embarrassment to many theologians, a word they would like to see dropped from our vocabulary. Yet there are also people who treat the notion of heresy in light-hearted fashion as a joke. Just as we chuckle over the prudishness of the Victorians, the notion of branding dissenters as heretics seems quaint. Some people even enjoy being called heretics. Will Herberg observes: "Today, people eagerly vaunt themselves as heretics, hoping that they will thereby prove interesting; for what does a heretic mean today but an original mind, a man who thinks for himself and spurns creeds and dogmas?"[1] Gerald Kennedy writes: "It has become something of a badge of honor to be regarded as a heretic, and most younger men who are discussing Christian theology and Christian ethics will pay as much attention to this label as they would to an accusation of being progressive."[2]

Those who discuss the concept of heresy like to point out that the Greek word from which we get our English term *heresy* originally meant choice. The heretic, it seems, is someone who chooses, who makes his own decisions and does not allow someone else to tell him what to think and what to do. If this is the case, then ours should be the great age of heresy, for we are able—indeed, forced—to make more choices than any generation before us. Peter Berger therefore speaks of the "heretical *imperative*":

> Modernity multiplies choices and concomitantly reduces the scope of what is experienced as destiny. In the matter of religion, as indeed in other areas of human life and thought, this means that the modern individual is faced not just with the opportunity but with the necessity to make choices as to his beliefs. This fact constitutes the heretical im-

> perative in the contemporary situation. Thus heresy, once the occupation of marginal and eccentric types, has become a much more general condition; indeed heresy has become universalized.[3]

Man has come of age: he must choose for himself. Heresy—understood as choice—is the fate and privilege of all modern men and women.

II

When heretics are discussed in our time, it is usually with considerable sympathy—often the sympathy we feel for an underdog. We may not agree with the heretic, but we wish him well. Thomas Szasz writes: ". . . so long as there is tension between the individual and the group of which he is a member, there will be heresy, whatever it might be called." What, then, is heresy? It is "being right when the right thing to do is to be wrong."[4] Shailer Mathews views heresy in similar terms: "Heresy is the belief of a defeated party. If it had succeeded it would have been orthodoxy."[5]

Some writers are eager to enlist respected historical figures under heresy's banner. Barrows Dunham argues: ". . . it is plain that the historical Jesus was in his time and place a heretic."[6] Walter Nigg speaks of "the inexplicable Christ" and argues: "With the revelation of Jesus as a heretic, we have at least made a beginning in the hard task of speaking about him in other than the hackneyed phrases which have lost all affective power."[7]

Heretics often get high marks for sincerity and are compared to saints. George Shriver writes: "Without a manual of church history as a program guide, it would be very difficult to tell the saints from the heretics in the course of Christian history. Both have been the most religious men of their own generations!"[8]

But the heretic is not always depicted as a saint: he may also be a politician struggling for power. Barrows Dunham claims that heresies are "ideas which disrupt an existing society in such a way as to change, or to threaten to change, the distribution of power within it."[9] We will see later that some scholars view heresy as mere dissent or disagreement, while others maintain that only dissenters who also engage in disruptive actions should be called heretics.

III

Scholars who speak well of heretics sometimes operate with a dialectical conception of the relation between heresy and orthodoxy. Just as there are thinkers who believe that evil is dialectically necessary in order that there be good (e.g. Hegel, Schleiermacher),[10] there are scholars who view heresy as dialectically necessary to the development of orthodoxy—and in this sense good.

Walter Nigg writes that heresy is "a necessary component of the life of the church." Heresy is the "*other side* of the Gospel." Hence we can say that ". . . heresy is Christianity, Christianity felt to its fullest intensity." We can take a hopeful attitude toward heresy because ". . . the Gospel holds potentialities which have not yet come to the surface."[11] Robert McAfee Brown maintains that there must be a place for "dangerous" ideas in the church:

> The compensating weight of heresy may be necessary from time to time to keep the listing ship of orthodoxy from foundering. If so, we can hazard the guess that God has a special kind of affection for heretics, and even that he raises them up to fulfill his purposes when his usual means have been hampered by human self-sufficiency.[12]

IV

Generally speaking, we can distinguish two main views of heresy in the literature. Traditional authors who think of heresy mainly in the context of the history of Christianity view the heretic as a dangerous man who will probably cause harm or damage if nothing is done to stop him. Authors oriented toward modernity, on the other hand, tend to view the heretic as a mere dissenter, an individual whose right to disagree must be respected since our society guarantees freedom of speech.

The difference between these two conceptions is reflected in the title of Sidney Hook's book *Heresy, Yes—Conspiracy, No*. Hook belongs to the modern camp and defines a heresy as "a set of unpopular ideas or opinions on matters of grave concern to the community." A conspiracy is a "movement which by secret, underground organization plays outside the rules of the game and seeks to subvert the institutions or processes that are part of the democratic system." Hook appeals for "the toleration of dissent, no matter how heretical, not the toleration of conspiracy, no matter what its disguise."[13]

Hook's book is actually less tolerant of heresy than it sounds, for the traditional notion of heresy includes what he calls "conspiracy." The heretic as traditionally understood stirs up discord and disrupts the life of the church, with the result that the church or the state eventually has to take action against him, just as today the democratic state must take action—as Hook freely admits—against "conspirators" who try to subvert the democratic process.

V

We have seen that modern commentators on heresy usually give the heretic the benefit of the doubt. Hans Küng calls for a "benign" interpretation of heresy and argues that we should be willing to credit the heretic with "good faith."[14] Robert Grosseteste, a medieval English churchman, would not have agreed with this advice, for he defined a heresy as "an opinion chosen by human perception contrary to holy Scripture, publicly avowed and obstinately defended."[15]

This conception of heresy was shared by the Reformers, who were themselves called heretics. Luther and Calvin did not glorify individualism and subjectivism, as one might be inclined to think from reading certain contemporary characterizations of Protestantism. Luther observed: "That is the peculiarity of all heretics, to believe that they have the spirit of God, and to know nothing of original sin."[16] Calvin likewise pointed to the sinful element in heresy:

> . . . Augustine is right in describing pride as the mother of all heresies. For there has never been a teacher of error who has not been brought to his downfall by perverted ambition . . . We shall find that all of them have been attacked by the disease of pride and have created intellectual tortures for themselves and others.[17]

According to these observers, heretics are arrogant and claim to "know it all." Thomas Molnar has compared them to utopian thinkers, that is, people who propose to substitute for the existing social order something entirely different of their own devising: "Although of many varieties, heretics have all displayed characteristics which may be found among utopians as well. The principal common characteristic is to become like God in the knowledge of good and evil (Genesis 3:5)."[18]

Abraham Kuyper goes a bit further yet and attributes deceit to the heretics. He describes them as people ". . . who act as though they are bringing the truth and who have also drawn a good deal of their wisdom from God's revelation but in the meantime have deliberately mixed it with what comes out of their own hearts or with the wisdom of the world and the lies of Satan."[19]

What comes through in these more traditional characterizations of heresy is that heresy is first of all sin. Indeed, it is apostasy, a falling away from God and His truth. Thus we do not describe someone who has never been exposed to the gospel and Christian teaching as a heretic; the pagans encountered on the mission field are not heretics. Unbelief is not to be equated with apostasy.

VI

One of the great misconceptions with regard to heresy is that it has to do merely with the views one holds. There is more involved: heresy manifests itself ultimately as a rejection of authority, of the norm for our faith and life. In a book on medieval heresy we read:

> . . . heresy was not just a matter of doctrine but also one of discipline—pertinacious error. The heretic was one who persisted in his mistake, refusing correction after his fault had been shown to him. It was for obduracy that he was finally punished after all efforts to make him abjure had failed. Consequently the test of heresy was a moral and practical one—willingness to submit . . .[20]

The names of Korah, Dathan and Abiram, the Israelites who rebelled against the authority of Moses and Aaron in the wilderness, are not often mentioned in books on heresy, but their story exemplifies what is usually at issue. Before the punishment struck the three rebels and their families, Moses declared: "Hereby you shall know that the Lord has sent me to do all these works, and that it has not been of my own accord" (Numbers 16:28). Korah, Dathan and Abiram had not simply registered a minority opinion: they had stirred up discord by their "heresy," their choice, their rejection of Moses' authority as the leader designated by God.

Heretics, then, are not just doubters or dissenters or original thinkers who come up with fresh ideas. They are ultimately to be regarded as rebels against divine authority who endanger themselves and others by their divisive, schismatic activities. That harsh action has often been taken against sowers of discord should not surprise us. It is one thing to doubt certain Christian teachings or interpretations of Bible passages, but quite another to attack Christian traditions and institutions as a self-appointed leader.

VII

Heresy, then, is not disagreement on minor matters or academic questions. When Christian theologians disagree on secondary issues, they do not—or should not—accuse each other of heresy. The question of heresy is always bound up with the question of authority, which is of course a major matter. James I. Packer writes: "The deepest cleavages in Christendom are doctrinal; and the deepest doctrinal cleavages are those which result from disagreement about authority."[21]

The ultimate authority or criterion for settling doctrinal disputes is God's Word—the Bible. But in the modern world, writes Benjamin B. Warfield, people look to science, philosophy and the critical method as the standard for truth. This difference on the question of authority helps us to define heresy and orthodoxy: "We are 'orthodox' when we account God's declaration in his Word superior to them (i.e. science, philosophy and the critical method), their interpreter, and their corrector. We are 'heretical' when we make them superior in point of authority to God's Word, its interpreter, and its corrector." Thus heresy is "wilfulness in doctrine."[22] Edward J. Carnell accordingly defines orthodoxy as "that branch of Christendom which limits the ground of religious authority to the Bible."[23]

One of the most famous heretics in American religious history was Charles A. Briggs, who was tried on a heresy charge in the Presbyterian Church in 1892 and suspended from the ministry a year later. Briggs, an Old Testament professor who wanted to introduce "higher criticism" to America, did *not* limit authority to the Bible but argued that ". . . Reason is a great fountain of divine authority . . ."[24]

Heresy rejects the position the Bible claims for itself; it relies on an outside authority and introduces alien influences into Christianity. Hence there is something to the suggestion that heresy is born when Biblical spirituality encounters a major outside force, such as the Greek mind with its powerful philosophical tradition. Tertullian apparently thought along these lines, for he wrote: "It is philosophy that supplies the heresies with their equipment . . . Heretics and philosophers perpend the same themes and are caught up in the same discussions."[25]

Concession to alien authority is the very essence of heresy, according to Warfield. He speaks of concession as the "high road" to heresy.[26] Thus the primary issue is not which of the various Christian doctrines is rejected or modified, or how radically it is modified.

VIII

Our word *heresy* comes from a Greek word that is used in the Bible: there are explicit warnings about heresy in the New Testament. But is it exclusively a New Testament phenomenon? Peter links heresy with the Old Testament theme of false prophecy: "False prophets also arose among the people, just as there will be false teachers among you, who will secretly bring in destructive heresies, even denying the Master who bought them . . ." (II Peter 2:1). Heretics, then, are the New Testament equivalent of the false prophets of the Old Testament.

It is sometimes suggested that the false prophecy of the Old Testament must be attributed to demonic inspiration. It is true in at least one sense that human sinfulness is linked to satan's inspiration and encouragement, but we need not have recourse to the transcendent world of angels and spirits to describe and characterize false prophecy: it is apostasy, sin. G. C. Aalders writes that the ultimate origin of false prophecy is enmity in the human heart against God's revelation: ". . . Scripture teaches us to view false prophecy in the first place as born of the sinful human heart, as a product of factors that lie within man himself; demonic operation may be accepted only as a more distant factor."[27]

Heresy and false prophecy must not be understood as an explicit and total repudiation of the God of the Bible; it is not utterly secular, atheistic Humanism. The heretic includes elements of the Christian revelation and of Christian teaching in his system of thought. Christ is not ignored but is assigned a significant place in Islam, Mormonism and various other faiths that have arisen in the wake of Christianity—not the place of honor He deserves as the Son of God but an important place nevertheless. The heretic—like satan himself—knows how to quote Scripture when it suits him. Hence the old proverb "Geen ketter zonder letter" (No heretic without a text).

When heresy is understood in this way, it must be related to syncretism, that is, the effort to combine or synthesize Biblical revelation or Christian teachings with other religious and philosophical doctrines. Syncretism, according to W. A. Visser 't Hooft, involves a "revolt against the uniqueness and concreteness of a revelation in history." Syncretism ". . . does not know of revelation in that sense of the word. It may speak of many revelations, but this very multiplicity shows that none of them are in any sense decisive and that none of them demand a definite commitment. So syncretism has no centre, no point of reference."[28] In earlier ages the Christian faith was synthesized with other religions and cults, and also with rational-philosophical outlooks. Today syncretism takes on various forms, including that of a synthesis between Christianity and the political ideologies that people in many parts of the world are willing to fight for and die for.[29]

IX

If heresy is to be understood as the fruit borne by syncretism or a synthesis of the gospel with alien spiritual currents, such as the modern mind with its roots in the Enlightenment, is liberal Christianity, especially its Protestant version, to be branded wholly heretical? This is a difficult and painful question, for it involves judging the motives and intentions of churchmen and theologians who claim to have acted in the spirit and best interests of Christianity.

It can at least be said that liberal Christianity is frankly and openly accommodationist, that it makes a virtual principle of concession. Harry Emerson Fosdick, a leading spokesman for the liberal cause, writes that liberalism became "a movement of adaptation and accommodation": "We were adjusting Christian thought to a secular culture. Unaware of the consequence, we made the secular culture paramount and standard." The purpose of the liberal movement, according to Fosdick, was

> . . . to adjust Christian thinking to modern knowledge. The liberal theology of my generation was not just unconsciously molded by contemporary philosophic, scientific and social pressures; it was consciously, deliberately, sometimes desperately trying to adapt Christian thought to, and harmonize it with, the intellectual culture of our time. That was the only way in which we could save our faith, and its achievement was a matter of life and death.[30]

Thomas Oden, a former liberal, takes a much sterner view of accommodation. He complains about "addictive accommodationism" and "a diarrhea of religious accommodation." "The central theme of contemporary theology," he informs us, "is accommodation to modernity. It is the underlying motif that unites the seemingly vast differences between existential theology, process theology, liberation theology, demythologization, and many varieties of liberal theology—all are searching for some more compatible adjustment to modernity."[31] Oden, in response, calls for an orthodoxy that dares to defy modernity (see pp. 91-2 above).

We see what is truly at stake with regard to heresy when we realize that the movement in the accommodationist direction is ultimately a movement toward Humanism, the modern outlook that blossomed in the Enlightenment but has its roots in the Greek mind with its commitment to rationality. The Humanist quest for rationality ultimately becomes a rejection of any external authority, as "heteronomy" (law imposed by another) is replaced by "autonomy" (man a law unto himself). And autonomy, writes Jerald C. Brauer, ". . . is the basis for what has come to be called secularism. Autonomy asserts the essential non-religiousness of all structures of life. The age or the world is to be understood completely on its own basis. Man and the world are the measure of all things."[32]

Once we drift away from the authority of God's Word, we are in danger of embracing a totally and explicitly anti-Christian outlook on life. The divine authority of God's revelation clashes with the human authority underlying the drive for autonomy. Man cannot serve two masters.

CHAPTER TEN

CONFESSIONAL UNITY

I

CHRISTIANS who regard unity as a norm and ideal are swimming against the stream, for our society is markedly individualistic. We romanticize individual choice and tend to look upon a person who subordinates his convictions or plans to others or to an institution as somehow lacking in integrity. Our obsession with self-realization fits in nicely with the pluralistic rhetoric of tolerance: each individual is beautiful and correct and morally praiseworthy in his (or her) own way. What's right for me may not be right for you. To each his own! Christian obedience and self-denial seem out of place in such an atmosphere.

The much lamented break-up of Christianity into what we now call "denominations" reflects the individualism of the Western world. In New Testament days there were some Christians who took pride in following Paul while others followed Apollos, and they were rebuked for it (see I Corinthians 3:4). The denominations today can assert their individuality by proudly following Calvin or Luther or Wesley or some other theological leader. Evangelists tell us to worship at the "church of our choice." Apparently we must find the church that best fits *our* needs and aspirations. Calvinism may be right for *me*, but perhaps *you* need an Arminian church to meet *your* aspirations.

The existence of denominational divisions is greatly to be regretted, as Christians now freely admit. Leonard Swidler observes: ". . . the division of the Church is a betrayal of Christ ('I pray, Father, that they may all be one . . .') and a scandal to the world ('. . . so that the world may believe')."[1] Yet these denominational divisions cannot simply be abolished by a decision made one fine day. They have developed and deepened over decades and generations, and it will take considerable time to overcome them.

Real Christian unity would bring all Christians into full ecclesiastical fellowship. In the meantime we should work for genuine unity *within* the denominations as well. But what is the tie that binds the members of a church or a denomination together? Do members of a denomination enjoy the same kind of unity as the members of a chess club?

II

The unity that should exist within a denomination can best be described as a *confessional* unity, a unity rooted in a common creed. The confession is what all of the church says together, the faith which the members profess jointly. It is a faith in the promises of the gospel, in the message of the Scriptures as expressed and interpreted in one or more creeds to which the denomination officially commits itself. Such creeds are often called "doctrinal standards."

This confessional unity should not be thought of as theological unity. We saw in Chapter 8 that there are differences between theology on the one hand and dogma or doctrine or creed on the other. Theology, as the result of scholarly activity, is more tentative than a creed. It is also more extensive and detailed. Theologians stake out positions on various matters on which the creeds do not rule.

Another important difference is that the creeds—or many of them, at least—have a more personal and existential character. The Heidelberg Catechism opens with the question: "What is your only comfort in life and death?" The answer is a moving statement of faith: "That I, with body and soul, both in life and death, am not my own, but belong unto my faithful Saviour Jesus Christ; who with His precious blood has fully satisfied for all my sins, and delivered me from the power of the devil . . ."[2] The Apostles' Creed is a statement of faith beautiful especially in its simplicity. It opens with the words: "I believe in God the Father, Almighty, Maker of heaven and earth, and in Jesus Christ, His only begotten Son, our Lord . . ." This creed is often repeated at the open grave as a statement of the believer's comfort and hope in the face of death.

III

Unity is elusive. Some denominations possess genuine confessional unity, but others permit—or even encourage—"theological pluralism." Still, few churches claim to be without unity. Some simply declare that they are united—without specifying how. Suggestions to the contrary are dismissed as uncharitable.

Perhaps the most interesting denominational tradition in this respect is the Church of England. It has been suggested that the Anglican churches around the world represent a "provisional prototype of the reunited *Ecumene,* the world-Christianity of the future."[3] Anglicans are not generally given to feuding and do not have many schisms in their history. In a book on Anglicanism "in ecumenical perspective" we read: "The principal and most characteristic feature of Anglicanism is moderation."[4] Stephen Neill seems to be getting at the same point when he talks about the indefinable quality of Anglican thought." He observes: "If the Church of England had not developed a capacity, unmatched in any other Christian communion in the world, for tolerating the intolerable, it would have been brought to an end long ago."[5] John W. Lawrence views the Anglican genius for keeping the peace as a gift: ". . . the special gift of the Anglican communion is the knowledge that some things, which have generally been thought to be incompatible, really belong together . . ."[6]

Not all commentators on Anglicanism take such a benign view of the Anglican "gift." John M. Krumm, for example, speaks of the "genius of Anglicanism for double-talk."[7] The unity achieved at such a price seems to many observers to be no unity at all. Yet there is more to the Anglican achievement than such criticism allows us to recognize. Stephen Sykes suggests that although there is "no specifically Anglican theory," there is an "Anglican practice."[8] The inclusiveness or comprehensiveness of the Anglican tradition does not guarantee much in the way of doctrinal uniformity, but there is indeed a certain admirable unity in worship and liturgy. (There is also considerable liturgical unity in Lutheran circles.)

The importance of this dimension of Christian unity is all too often overlooked. Because Christians engage in public worship so often that it seems commonplace, various features of worship rarely become the object of explicit reflection. How is God to be addressed and spoken of in the worship service? How are we to speak of Christ? What, exactly, is public communal prayer? What is going on when the congregation partakes of the Lord's supper or communion? Unity in these matters—even a unity rooted largely in tradition—should not be taken lightly. We rarely stop to think about it, but such unity by itself represents a significant form of confessional unity. The same can be said about church government, which is why it is unfortunate when congregations in a denomination insist on going their own way in matters of worship and liturgy and church order. Christian unity is eroded in the process.

IV

The Anglican emphasis on unity in liturgy and church order indicates that unity can be sought in non-doctrinal agreement. It happens that many Christians of our time pin their hopes for unity mainly on the non-doctrinal side of Christianity. Those who do so love to use the word *orthopraxis* (or *orthopraxy*), which is then contrasted with *orthodoxy*. Unity, it appears, is to be sought more in right conduct than in right teaching. Hans Küng writes: "If remaining in the truth is essentially a question of discipleship in the Spirit of Jesus Christ, this is *more a matter of orthopraxy than of orthodoxy*: it is realized more in the Christian life than in teaching, more in the deed than merely in the word."[9]

The emphasis on orthopraxis is not simply an effort to dispense with the concern for truth, then. The question is which conception of truth we should embrace. Küng offers us a contrast: "The truth of Christianity is not something to be 'contemplated,' 'theorized,' but to be 'done,' 'practiced.' The Christian concept of truth is not—like the Greek—contemplative-theoretical, but operative-practical."[10] This is essentially the conception of truth we find in various liberation theologians, who are deeply influenced by the elevation of "praxis" over "theory" in much contemporary thinking. José Miguez Bonino tells us that "action is itself the truth." Praxis is not led by theory or knowing: "Correct knowledge is contingent on right doing. Or rather, the knowledge is disclosed in the doing." Thus Christian praxis is not normed or judged by some confessional standard external to itself. We read: ". . . there is no possibility of invoking or availing oneself of a norm outside praxis itself."[11]

This way of thinking is not as new as is sometimes supposed. What it basically boils down to can be neatly expressed by way of a slogan that has been with us for decades: "Deeds, not creeds." The liberalism or modernism of the first half of our century did not use the term *orthopraxis*, but it promoted the same emphasis—unity through *agenda* (i.e. what is to be done) rather than through *credo* (i.e. what we believe).

Shailer Mathews, one of the leading spokesmen for modernism, argued: "Behavior and attitudes . . . are the very essence of a religion and the methods by which they are intellectually justified are relative to one's intelligence." Theology, declared Mathews, is "functional."[12] Hence he called for a "de-theologizing of the Christian movement."[13]

In the face of such statements, we can understand why J. Gresham Machen, the opponent of the modernists, complained about "the passionate anti-intellectualism of the Modernist Church" and called modernism "a movement which really degrades the intellect by excluding it from the sphere of religion." In this regard modernism was keeping pace with the modern world, argued Machen: "The depreciation of the intellect, with the exaltation in place of it of the feelings or of the will, is, we think, a basic fact in modern life, which is rapidly leading to a condition in which men neither know anything nor care anything about the doctrinal content of the Christian religion, and in which there is in general a lamentable intellectual decline."[14]

V

The Christian tradition has by no means been oblivious to the problem raised in the debate about orthodoxy and orthopraxis. The New Testament writers already addressed this issue in terms of the question of faith and works: "Be doers of the word, and not hearers only" (James 1:22). "For as the body apart from the spirit is dead, so faith apart from works is dead" (2:26). Here the New Testament was echoing the Old. H. M. Kuitert writes: "The Old Testament knows no sharp distinction between word and deed, any more than between speaking and acting."[15]

Unsympathetic commentators on Christianity often misconstrue this point and suggest that Christians regard themselves as saved on account of their orthodoxy. Barrows Dunham writes:

"Faith justifies, Luther had said, and Calvin after him; works (that is to say, actions) do not. Or, to turn theological language into philosophical: a right theory as to fact and morals is sufficient to the good life."[16]

Such misinterpretations of Christianity usually result from an identification of the notion of scientific theory, which is a relatively late development in Western history, with doctrine or creed. Under the influence of intellectualism and scientism, it is assumed that if Christianity has specific teachings, these are to be regarded as its "theories." But creeds and doctrines are not essentially theological or theoretical in character, as we have seen. They are not abstract and tentative, and they can be closely related to daily life. In other words, the separation between doctrine and life, or between "orthodoxy" and "orthopraxis," is foreign to the Bible and to genuine Christian spirituality. When the psalmist prays, "Teach me thy way, O Lord," what he is asking for is not theory or science but concrete guidance and direction for daily life, as we can see from how he completes his sentence: "Teach me thy way, O Lord, that I may walk in thy truth" (Psalm 86:11).

VI

We must be careful, however, not to simply *equate* doctrine and life, "orthodoxy" and "orthopraxis." Although the Bible does not separate them, regarding them rather as intimately related, it does recognize that doctrine comes first in a significant sense. Doctrine or our confession is God-given. We saw earlier (p. 29 above) that "What think ye of the Christ?" is the question of the ages. When Jesus put this question to Peter by asking him, "Who do you say that I am?" he responded with a stirring confession: "You are the Christ, the Son of the living God." Jesus then declared: "Blessed are you, Simon, Bar-Jonah! For flesh and blood has not revealed this to you, but my Father, who is in heaven" (Matthew 16:15-17).

Martin Luther no doubt had such considerations in mind when he argued that doctrine and life must be distinguished (which is not to say that they should be separated). "Doctrine belongs to God," wrote Luther, "not to us; and we are called only as its ministers." He formulated this point even more dramatically by arguing: "Doctrine is heaven; life is earth." The upshot of the matter is that purity of doctrine should be our special concern. Luther pointed out:

> . . . we do not permit the slightest offense against it. But we can be lenient toward errors of life. For we, too, err daily in our life and conduct; so do all the saints, as they earnestly confess in the Lord's Prayer and the Creed. But by the grace of God our doctrine is pure; we have all the articles of faith solidly established in Sacred Scripture.[17]

This distinction between doctrine and life is fundamental to understanding the most famous and most quoted statement of Luther's colorful life—his "Here I stand" speech before the Diet of Worms in 1521, where he was asked to justify his course of action. In this speech he clearly distinguished his conduct or life from the doctrine he was defending, which he had found in Scripture: "For I do not make myself out to be any kind of saint, nor am I now contending about my conduct but about Christian doctrine."[18]

We find essentially the same point being made by Calvin: Christian doctrine is given by God and must not be confused with human opinion. Calvin tells us that God ". . . puts a perpetual distinction between the human mind and the revelation of his Spirit. If this be so, it follows that what men utter of themselves is a perverse fiction, because the Spirit of God claims to himself alone, as we have said, the office of showing what is true and right."[19] And what is found in Calvin is generally found in Bavinck as well: "In essence, all the truths of the Christian faith come to man from the outside. They are known to him only through revelation, and they become his possession only when he accepts them like a child in faith."[20]

If Christian truth is ultimately God-given, there is no room for Paul Tillich's accusation that orthodoxy represents "intellectual pharisaism."[21] Any claim that one's *life* or *conduct* is upright and correct might well be regarded as pharisaical, but the doctrine we profess is not ours in the same sense as our conduct. Doctrine belongs to God; it is God's truth!

VII

The emphasis on orthopraxis is also mistaken for another reason: it is strangely out of step with Christian spirituality. Should the Christian be identified with what he *does*, as opposed to what he believes and *confesses*? Critics of Christianity usually say yes, and then are quick to point to the inevitable gap between the Christian's confession and his conduct. Since there is such a gap in the life of every Christian, it appears that all Christians are hypocrites, people who fail to practice what they preach.

The fear of being accused of hypocrisy leads many Christians to be rather subdued about their confession. But a mature Christian spirituality recognizes something liberating and exhilarating in the very gap that leads to the hypocrisy charge: God's abounding grace gives him hope. The believer refuses to identify himself with his actions, his sins, for he confesses them to God and thereby puts them behind him. He then pledges to live by the law of God, which is a pledge he never fully lives up to. But in confessing his sins and affirming his love for God's law, he moves beyond his sinfulness and reaches forward to take hold of a new and better future. "O how I love thy law! It is my meditation all the day" (Psalm 119:97). The believer strains and does his utmost to attain that better future: "Let us also lay aside every weight, and sin which clings so closely, and let us run with perseverance the race that is set before us, looking to Jesus the pioneer and perfecter of our faith" (Hebrews 12:1-2).

The Christian confession, then, is forward-moving in character. That's why the believer identifies himself with his confession, his *credo*, rather than his actions, which he leaves behind him as unneeded baggage. Sin and our past must be renounced: this is part of what we mean by self-denial. We transcend our history of sin and failure as we strive to meet our solemn pledge and commitment. The Christian does not say, "I *am* my history, my deeds." Rather, he wants to be identified in terms of his promise, his commitment to dedicate his life to Christ.

What applies to the individual believer applies also to the congregation, to the assembly of God's people. The members of the congregation are bound to one another not first of all in ethnic or linguistic or cultural respects or even because they share a common history: their unity is confessional in nature. *Together* they confess their sin, and *together* they renew their pledge to reach forward toward a fuller realization of God's promises. To say that they are confessionally united does not mean that they all hold the same opinions but that they have made a joint commitment. That's why a worship service must never be conceived of as a situation in which a preacher entertains an audience; genuine congregational participation is essential. Worship binds the members of the congregation to one another and to their God.

VIII

We see, then, that confessional unity is not a simple given to be taken for granted but something the congregation works toward. In other words, there is growth in unity, for different degrees of unity are possible. And what applies to the local congregation also applies to the church in a larger sense. The various parts and wings of the church must look to creeds and doctrines as the basis for genuine unity, and if doctrinal division appears they must work to overcome it.

The disagreements that arise are sometimes superseded in history, for doctrinal development does take place. There were already disputes between Peter and Paul during the apostolic age, but they were resolved in time. Roman Catholicism makes much of the notion of development, arguing that while the truth remains essentially the same, there is growth in the church's *consciousness of the truth*, a growth that is sometimes described as a movement from the implicit to the explicit. John Henry Newman (1801-90), a convert to Catholicism who eventually became a cardinal, gave classic expression to this notion, arguing

> . . . that, from the nature of the human mind, time is necessary for the full comprehension and perfection of great ideas; and that the highest and most wonderful truths, though communicated to the world once for all by inspired teachers, could not be comprehended all at once by the recipients, but, as being received and transmitted by minds not inspired and through media which were human, have required only the longer time and deeper thought for their full elucidation.[22]

Protestantism also recognizes the development of dogma. James Orr, the author of a major book on the subject, writes:

> I believe . . . that, so far from the history of dogma being the fatuous, illusory thing that many people suppose, there is a true law and logic underlying its progress, a true divine purpose and leading in its developments, a deeper and more complete understanding of Christianity in its many-sided relations being wrought out by its labours; and that, while its advance has not been without much conflict, much error, much implication with human sin and infirmity, and is yet far from complete, that advance has in the main been onward, and has

> yielded results which further progress will not subvert, any more than the future developments of science will subvert, say, such discoveries as the circulation of the blood, or the law of gravitation.[23]

The notion of development, of course, is by no means foreign to the modern mind, which is infatuated with evolution. Thus there are also thinkers who interpret doctrinal development along historicist lines and argue that the norm for the development cannot possibly lie at the beginning but must be sought in the *telos*, the end. (Here we see the influence of Hegel.) Robert Wilken takes such an approach and maintains—contrary to Newman and Orr—that Scripture may not be regarded as normative for doctrinal development: "The New Testament represents a 'random' selection from the Christian tradition as it had developed by the end of the first one or two generations." Wilken complains: "By idealizing the apostolic period, i.e. a particular historical epoch in the past, Christians have prized as values tradition, antiquity, apostolicity, uniformity, and permanence, and they have spurned change, innovation, novelty, and diversity."[24]

Wilken stands for the modern ideal of ceaseless change, permanent flux, in which, it appears, there are no limits to what something may develop or evolve into. We cannot speak of the "essence" of Christianity: we must see what it becomes. G. K. Chesterton opposes this mentality by means of his conception of man as the "animal that makes dogmas." He writes:

> As he piles doctrine on doctrine and conclusion on conclusion in the formation of some tremendous scheme of philosophy and religion, he is, in the only legitimate sense of which the expression is capable, becoming more and more human. When he drops one doctrine after another in a refined skepticism, when he declines to tie himself to a system, when he says that he has outgrown definitions, when he says that he disbelieves in finality, when, in his own imagination, he sits as God, holding no form of creed but contemplating all, then he is by that very process sinking slowly backwards into the vagueness of the vagrant animals and the unconsciousness of the grass. Trees have no dogmas. Turnips are singularly broad-minded.[25]

IX

If there is to be genuine growth toward greater confessional unity through doctrinal development, Christians must be willing to learn. In other words, they must be careful not to *equate* their own opinions and views with God's truth but must instead admit that they may have to be corrected by Scripture or by their fellow Christians. And if such learning is to take place, there must be historical awareness. In this regard, the "Christian amnesia" that seems to afflict so many believers, cutting them off from the church's past, is a serious problem (see p. 92 above).

To be historically aware, we must be willing to examine past doctrines and ideas in context and must take the trouble to find out what questions were in the minds of the church's leaders when certain doctrines were formulated and certain statements made (see p. 34 above). Here the infatuation with the modern mind that has stricken so many Christians is a definite problem, for it leads them to turn their back on their Christian heritage and renders their thinking vulnerable to non-Christian and even anti-Christian emphases. It is no accident that the cults are making such inroads in Christian circles. James Hitchcock points out:

> The demythologizing first of dogma, then of Scripture; the tendency to see ethical behavior as the only genuine criterion of real Christianity; the habit of continually reformulating Christian teaching to get rid of its "outmoded" elements; the instinctive acceptance of prevailing cultural assumptions as normative for faith; and the willingness to regard good will and sincerity among men as all that ultimately matters combine to encourage the slow disappearance of anything like a distinctive Christianity in visible continuity with the church over two thousand years and thereby render Christians vulnerable to any religious movement which seems to possess the aggressive vitality their own church lacks.[26]

Our time sorely needs the kind of doctrinal development that could lead to a major restatement of the Christian faith in which it is set off first of all from the modern mind with its roots in the Enlightenment and in the commitment to rationality among the Greeks, and secondly from the various cults, sects and religions which are growing in influence in our time. But such a statement, that is, the formulation of a major new creed, would presuppose definite growth toward confessional unity, and such growth simply has not taken place. J. Gresham Machen considered this need decades ago and concluded sadly that "ours is not a creed-making age." He wrote: ". . . I think such doctrinal advance to be just now extremely unlikely. We are living in a time of widespread intellectual as well as moral decadence, and the visible church has unfortunately not kept free from this decadence."[27] Have things changed for the better since Machen's time? If anything, the confusion has increased.

X

Even if our time is not ripe for the promulgation of a new creed that will make it clear for our circumstances what Christianity is and is not, the work of doctrinal definition can and should proceed. And definition, if it is to amount to anything, involves exclusion. But what is to be excluded? Does Christianity include liberalism or modernism? Must we contend for the faith by disbarring liberalism, or must the borders within which Christianity is enclosed be enlarged?

It was this very question that led Machen to embroil himself in so much controversy. He could not promulgate a new creed on his own and expect to have it accepted, but he certainly could address this issue. Thus he wrote:

> The plain fact is, disguised though it be by the use of traditional language, that two mutually exclusive religions are contending for the control of the Church today. One is the great redemptive religion known as Christianity; the other is the naturalistic or agnostic Modernism . . . A separation between the two is the crying need of the hour; that separation alone can bring Christian unity.[28]

His best-known book was devoted to this subject—*Christianity and Liberalism.* He argued: ". . . despite the liberal use of traditional phraseology, modern liberalism not only is a different religion from Christianity but belongs in a totally different class of religions."[29]

Such language clearly represents intolerance in some sense—the intolerance of the Bible itself. A. A. van Ruler writes: "There is no more intolerant book in the world than the New Testament. It says that the truth is given, that it lies behind us, in one name, one person, one event."[30]

Genuine tolerance is not to be sought in a commitment to liberal ideals, for liberalism can show itself to be amazingly intolerant of its opponents. Neither is tolerance to be grounded in the gentle relativism that we today call pluralism, for relativism gradually leads to anarchy, which is finally replaced by a repressive authoritarianism when the disorder grows too great. Tolerance is ultimately rooted in the divine command—not in human good will or in skepticism and despair about truth. Genuine tolerance requires a recognition that we are not the *possessors* of truth but *witnesses* to *God's* truth. Hendrik Kraemer describes this recognition as the "apostolic attitude," for it leads us to invite others to accept and submit to the truth as well.[31] But any such submission requires spiritual change, and thus a free decision.

Tolerance creates room for freedom and therefore should be regarded not as part of the heritage of liberalism and relativism but as one of God's good gifts. God wants human beings to have time and room and opportunity to rise to their calling as the crown of creation living in fellowship with Him and caring for the world He made. Van Ruler explains:

> The God of the Bible leaves man the greatest conceivable elbow-room (*speelruimte*). A state with the Bible is under an obligation imposed by God to exercise the greatest possible tolerance. Thus tolerance enjoys divine sanction. Unless I am mistaken, the Biblical understanding of existence is the only all-embracing conception in which tolerance actually fits in such an organic manner and to its deepest depths.[32]

There are important differences between spiritual tolerance and political tolerance. What the state tolerates, the church is not necessarily obliged to tolerate. And there are other institutions and organizations to be considered as well, such as Christian educational institutions. Thus we turn now to a new set of questions involving Christian institutions.

PART FOUR

CHRISTIAN INSTITUTIONS

INDIVIDUALS contend for the faith, but we tend to forget that institutions do so as well. The story of Martin Luther's battle against the Roman Catholic Church is told and retold, but most Christians prefer not to talk about the medieval Inquisition, which was in effect a Christian institution doing battle for the faith in its own way. Thus there are some further questions to be raised.

First of all, despite the widespread recognition that Christian—or perhaps religious—unity is an ideal to be striven for, there is little agreement on the basis for such unity and the means by which it is to be achieved. In other words, we need to face the question of ecumenism (Chapter 11). Ecumenism involves not just individuals but churches and other institutions as well. Thus it appears that institutions, like individuals, can have and maintain a Christian identity (Chapter 12). Institutions receive a good deal of criticism in our society because they seem by their very nature to impose certain restrictions on our freedom. Thus we must deal with the question of doctrinal and academic freedom (Chapter 13). Finally, Christianity can never take its place in any society for granted but must ever be ready to defend itself in appropriate ways. We call the defense of the faith apologetics (Chapter 14).

CHAPTER ELEVEN

THE CHALLENGE OF ECUMENISM

I

THE commitment to ecumenism is an ecclesiastical—or perhaps more broadly religious—quest for unity. And unity, in our anxious and troubled world, is accepted as a deep need, for mankind is threatened with destruction. Andrei Sakharov, a Russian scientist and dissident intellectual, writes:

> The division of mankind threatens it with destruction. Civilization is imperiled by: a universal thermonuclear war, catastrophic hunger for most of mankind, stupefaction from the narcotic of "mass culture," and bureaucratized dogmatism, a spreading of mass myths that put entire peoples and continents under the power of cruel and treacherous demagogues, and destruction or degeneration from the unforeseeable consequences of swift changes in the conditions of life on our planet.
>
> In the face of these perils, any action increasing the division of mankind, any preaching of the incompatibility of world ideologies and nations is madness and a crime.[1]

This awareness of the importance of unity has roots in precommunist Russian history. In his story about the "Grand Inquisitor," Dostoevsky speaks of "the craving for universal unity" and the desire of mankind to unite in "one unanimous and harmonious ant-heap."[2] We are reminded of the tower of Babel, which is described for us as a "tower with its top in the heavens" (Genesis 11:4).

The failure of Christians in our time to achieve unity among themselves—to say nothing of a broader unity involving non-Christians as well—is widely regarded as "scandalous," as a barrier to Christian effectiveness. H. Richard Niebuhr writes: "The history of schism has been a history of Christianity's defeat. The church which began its career with the promise of peace and brotherhood for a distracted world has accepted the divisions in the society it had hoped to transform and has championed the conflicts it had thought to transcend."[3]

Various thinkers view identification with society or absorption by society as the key to the problem. Christianity has compromised itself especially by its close relationship with Western civilization. W. A. Visser 't Hooft therefore argues that the ". . . interpretation which considered Christianity as an ingredient of Western civilization and missions as an instrument of Western cultural penetration was itself the product of a relativistic and superficial approach to the fundamental issues of truth."[4] As Western civilization finds itself confronting the rising non-Western nations with aspirations of their own, the image of Christianity as the religion of the West is proving an obstacle to worldwide Christian unity.

II

Unity is not the only strongly felt need of our time: another is certainty. What makes our current situation so difficult is that these two needs often seem incompatible. Our certainties create disunity, and when we put unity first we seem to have little room left for deeply held convictions.

One traditional way of dealing with this tension is to declare that there must be more than one road to truth. The fourth-century Roman statesman Symmachus, who was a proponent of paganism and an opponent of Christianity, declared:

> Why should not all live in peace and harmony? We look up at the same stars, we are fellow passengers on the same planet and dwell beneath the same sky. What matters it along which road each individual endeavors to find the ultimate truth? The riddle of existence is too great that there should be only one road leading to an answer.[5]

What this means theologically is that there is more than one road to salvation. Hans Küng writes that the non-Christian religions must now be recognized as "ways of salvation" for many people: ". . . there is salvation outside the Church. In addition to particular, there can be seen a general, universal salvation history."[6] Wilfred Cantwell Smith concurs, identifying all of human history with salvation history:

> All human history is *Heilsgeschichte*. The most important missionary task of the Church, at least of its missionary leaders, is probably to lead the Church to seeing this so as to enable it to respond, so that Christians may participate, not fortuitously or ineptly, but intelligently and Christianly in the salvation history of all people.[7]

Another way of dealing with the tension between unity and certainty is syncretism, the effort to combine or synthesize various different religious traditions and principles, just as the Israelites in the days of Elijah and Ahab wanted to combine the worship of Jehovah with the worship of Baal.[8] Syncretism, of course, presupposes that the religions standing over against one another make no claim to exclusive truth. Hence Visser 't Hooft writes that syncretism ". . . can only bring together the religions which do not believe in specific, concrete revelation."[9] Various Oriental religions are open to synthesis with other religions, but Christianity is not: as a religion of revelation, it resists any fusion with other religions.

The syncretist solution to the tension between unity and certainty presupposes that religion as such is inherently good and that all religions should therefore be favorably disposed toward one another, just as dedicated chess players have something in common and can understand one another in their fascination with this ancient game. But this presupposition is highly questionable. Elton Trueblood argues: "The notion that religion is intrinsically a good thing will not bear examination at all, for some religions, judged by their effect upon human lives, are radically evil."[10]

Finally, it is questionable whether religions can be combined at all. Are religions made up of atoms or building blocks that can be separated and put together in new ways? Hendrik Kraemer argues against an atomistic approach and claims that we must ". . . take a religion as one whole body of religious life and expression, of which all the component parts are inseparably interrelated to each other and animated by the same apprehension of the totality of existence peculiar to it." He further explains:

> . . . religion is nowhere in the world an assortment of spiritual commodities, that can be compared as shoes or neck-ties. This sounds frivolous, nevertheless it is a point of such overwhelming importance that it can hardly be over-estimated. It ought never to be forgotten in the treatment of religious subjects—but it constantly is—that religion

> is the vast and desperate effort of mankind to get somehow an apprehension of the totality of existence, and therefore every religion is an indivisible, and not to be divided, unity of existential apprehension. It is not a series of tenets, dogmas, prescriptions, institutions, practices, that can be taken over one by one as independent items of religious life, conception or organization, and that can arbitrarily be compared with, and somehow related to, and grafted upon the similar item of another religion.[11]

III

Another factor in the tension between unity and certainty is the Christian claim about the centrality of Jesus Christ and of God's revelation to Israel. Commentators on Christianity sometimes speak of a "scandal of particularity"; it seems somehow arbitrary and unreasonable that God should reveal Himself to one nation in the ancient world, and not to others. And if only one, why the Hebrews rather than the cultivated Greeks? Furthermore, why was the time of the Roman empire favored with the incarnation? Wouldn't our age with its awesome network of communications have been more suitable? Kraemer writes: "The opinion is often heard that it would be detestable pride on the part of a Christian and a sample of mean thinking about God to suppose that He has 'limited' His revelation to Israel and left the other peoples destitute."[12]

Various thinkers proclaim that the time for such an outlook is over. Wilfred Cantwell Smith rejects the "exclusivist position" and "religious isolationism." From a church document he quotes a sentence that greatly disturbs him: "Without the particular knowledge of God in Jesus Christ, men do not really know God at all." He dismisses any such claim as "arrogant" and "intolerant" and unworthy of a Christian.[13] Brian Hebblethwaite talks about "the absence of a single starting point in the epistemology of religion." He advises: ". . . we cannot remain uncritically within the horizon of a single tradition . . . Above all, we have to ask ourselves whether the unique and allegedly normative elements in any one particular tradition can really maintain their universality in a pluralistic religious world."[14]

Theologians have developed a vehicle for relating various different religious traditions to Christianity to overcome the "scandal" of Christianity's claim to exclusive truth. The Old Testament, as we saw earlier (pp. 70-1 above), serves as background and interpretive context for the Christ event and the revelation given in the New Testament. The early Christian apologists already suggested that the glories of Greek civilization (especially the philosophy of Plato) could be regarded as a providential preparation for the gospel. Greek philosophy would then be the background against which the New Testament is to be understood. Central to this development is the conception of the universal Logos developed by Justin Martyr (c. 100-165), which he then identified with the Word (Greek: *logos*) of John 1. All men receive the truth by way of the Logos, according to Justin. Avery Dulles comments: "Justin's doctrine of the universal Logos was to have an important future in helping theologians from Clement and Origen to Tillich and K. Rahner to relate Christianity to the other religions . . ."[15] Greek philosophy, according to Clement of Alexandria, was a pedagogue or "schoolmaster" used by God ". . . to bring the Hellenic mind, as the law brings the Hebrews, 'to Christ.' "[16]

The model established here by the early apologists can be applied to thinkers and religious leaders of all sorts and has been used to build many bridges to and from Christianity. The universal Logos then functions as the "anonymous Christ" (see pp. 21-2 above) who reveals His name to certain people at a particular time and place in history but is at the same time active in all the nations leading them to truth. Hans Küng writes:

> According to the Christian theology of the second century (especially Justin) and the third (especially the Alexandrians Clement and Origen), the divine Logos (*logos spermatikos*, "seminal word") was active everywhere from the beginning. But if the pagans Plato, Aristotle and Plotinus, or later—for others—even Marx and Freud could be "pedagogues" leading men to Christ, why not also the philosophers and religious thinkers of other nations? Does not the East offer forms of thought and organization, structures and models, within which Christianity could be conceived and lived just as easily as in Western forms?[17]

Missionaries of our time have begun to relate non-Christian religious traditions to the New Testament as alternative Old Testaments, in effect, which then serve as pedagogues or schoolmasters to prepare the people in their part of the world for the gospel. In this way it becomes possible to combine the various religions of the world: in time, presumably, the anonymous Christ would become fully known to those among whom He has worked unrecognized. Hendrik Kraemer writes that various Christians and missionaries with a "more or less relativist conception of Christianity" have thought along such lines. The result was that ". . . the doctrine that the 'sacred oracles' of the great non-Christian religions are the Old Testaments of China, India, etc., and validly take the place of the Jewish Old Testament as the document of the *praeparatio evangelica* [preparation for the gospel], easily found support." The question that Kraemer raises in the face of this development is ". . . where the unity of the Christian Church would remain if all religious and cultural heritages became the special Old Testaments of the various Christian Churches."[18]

IV

The type of Christianity or world-religion that would emerge from such a global synthesis might be expected to be truly tolerant. Yet a paradox confronts us here: the most tolerant people and points of view sometimes turn out to be surprisingly intolerant. Paul Sudhakar, an evangelist to the Hindus, observes: "Hinduism is tolerant, but Hindus are intolerant of the exclusiveness of the Christian preacher." He explains: "Hindu tolerance is based upon a philosophical principle that truth is never the monopoly of one religion, that there are different ways of knowing truth, that God can be known in many ways."[19]

We see, then, that tolerance is not always what it appears to be. Elton Trueblood argues: "Carried to its logical limit . . . the principle of absolute toleration would prohibit all evangelism."[20] If all religious points of view are equally valid, appeals to change one's religion are not needed. This was apparently the conviction of M. K. Gandhi, who helped lead India to independence. Gandhi declared:

> Current missionary activities are of three kinds, good works, education and religious propaganda. In the India of tomorrow the first two will be allowed to go on without hindrance and will even be welcome but, if the missionaries continue to bend their efforts towards religious proselytizing through medical and educational work and so on, I shall

> certainly insist that they leave free India. The religions of India are right for her people: we have no need of spiritual conversion.[21]

Hendrik Kraemer comments that Gandhi's "fundamental relativism" turns out to be a "militant absolutism." He explains: "Gandhi's notion about religions is that they are products of the national soil . . . and that therefore it is incumbent on everyone to keep to his 'national' religion. The universal character of real religion and the problem of truth are entirely disregarded in this conception . . ."[22]

The restricted conception of mission work which Gandhi was prepared to tolerate has unfortunately been adopted by various missionary agencies. Christians who put orthopraxis in the place of orthodoxy tend to turn mission work into a medical, social, economic, and political program for the betterment of society as a whole. Hence it has been charged that ecumenical emphases and the prominence of the ecumenical movement are responsible for the "demise of evangelism."[23]

Central to the reorientation in missions is the concept of "humanization," which enables missionaries to work for change without confronting people with the choice for or against Christ. Peter Beyerhaus writes that he is dismayed ". . . to see how naively current ecumenical missiology can take up the concept of humanization and put it one-sidedly into the center of its motivation and goal." The scandal of the gospel is avoided, as the concept of humanization helps us ". . . to find a field of common concern with Hindus, Moslems, Marxists and Humanists. For, according to the concept of the anonymous Christ *extra muros Ecclesiae* [outside the walls of the church] we are already sharing in Christ if we together with them work for the humanization of mankind."[24]

V

It is no accident that our age, in which we witness so much confusion and disagreement about the meaning of the Christian faith, has a lively interest in Christology. All sorts of perspectives on Christ are being offered to us today. Sad to say, the question "Who is Jesus Christ?" is something of an embarrassment to worldwide ecumenism. James Hitchcock writes:

> An ecumenism which began by asserting proudly that fidelity to Christ was alone the test of the true Christian, not adherence to the doctrines of a particular church, would end by finding Christ merely one more sectarian obstacle to unity. A good will embracing the entire human race would emerge as the only necessary common denominator.[25]

The exclusive Christ is removed as a barrier by being turned into either the "anonymous Christ" (functioning like Justin's universal Logos) or a mere human teacher and example for us—one of the great men of the ages.

"What think ye of the Christ?" is the key question in religion and life. And Christian unity must have Christ at its center. The New Testament tells us: "Every spirit which confesses that Jesus Christ has come in the flesh is of God, and every spirit which does not confess Jesus is not of God" (I John 4:2-3). Christ is essential to Christianity.

There are Christians who admit this but then offer us a strange recipe for Christian unity—"No creed but Christ." Wouldn't this overcome all the differences between Christians? Anyone with a good knowledge of church history and the various disputes about the two natures of Christ and the relation of Christ to the Father (see Chapter 2 above) cannot help but dismiss such an approach as too simple. It is indeed a wonderful thing to pledge allegiance to Jesus Christ, but one must still be able to say who He is. Was He a Jewish religious genius, or was He God incarnate?

Specific Christian doctrine is often divisive. A self-conscious Calvinist has undeniable doctrinal differences with Lutherans, Arminians, and so forth. This state of affairs makes some Christians uncomfortable. They then declare that they are Christians in a non-specific sense, neither Calvinist nor Lutheran nor Arminian—just Christian.

Children may be able to get by with being "just Christian" since they have not yet reflected seriously on the doctrinal points that divide Christians into creedal camps. For adults, however, it's not quite so simple. A mature, educated Christian must take some position or other on doctrinal issues, just as I have to wear a shirt of a certain color if I am to wear a shirt at all. I might want to avoid red and green and blue so as not to offend people who don't like those colors, but in the end I must make a choice. There are no shirts that are completely neutral with regard to color. The doctrinal traditions within Christianity are specific in much the same way.

VI

If ecumenism is truly our goal and norm, we will not let the inevitable doctrinal differences rule out fellowship with Christians of other traditions, although it will surely hinder it somewhat. Ecumenism takes place on a personal, individual level when Christians in a certain neighborhood, representing various different churches, form a Bible study group together, or join in some way to be of Christian service.

It is important to note that the basis for the unity that is then achieved is not a common set of opinions or views on doctrinal matters. Indeed, when Christians seek one another out, there may be considerable difference between them with regard to doctrine. What holds such Christians together and makes it possible for them to feel one is that Christ has claimed them all for His own. The ultimate bond of unity is oneness in relation to Christ. Naturally, this is not to say that confessional unity cannot serve to strengthen Christian fellowship. The point is simply that Christ's claim on the believer takes priority. That's why fellowship is possible between Christians with markedly different convictions.

VII

To emphasize ecumenism in this sense is to admit to a certain relativity in one's beliefs and doctrines. This is what the Calvinist does when he recognizes the Lutheran as a sincere believer and seeks fellowship with him. There are significant differences between Calvinism and Lutheranism, some of which have to do with Christology, but those differences should be regarded as open for discussion. The Calvinist naturally believes that the Lutheran is wrong on certain points, but he is willing to learn from him.

This openness must not be understood as relativism in the usual twentieth-century sense. The Calvinist regards his beliefs as relative and subject to change because they must always be tested against the ultimate, unchanging standard of God's Word, the unnormed norm. If the Lutheran can use the Bible to show the Calvinist that there are misconceptions or errors in his system of beliefs, change will be called for.

Such discussion should be regarded as genuinely ecumenical.

Different groups within the body of Christ talk together in an effort to learn from one another. They do not enter the discussion by forsaking their convictions but carry those convictions along, willing at every point to subject them to the standard of God's Word, which relativizes all our opinions and calls us to be tolerant of the convictions of other believers who claim to ground their views in Scripture.

If the convictions of believers are to be changed, it must be by persuasion and not by force. A Calvinist professor may not require of a Lutheran student that he agree with the Calvinist position, but it is reasonable to expect the Lutheran student to be able to state the Calvinist position and to be acquainted with the historical factors that helped to shape it. The doctrinal differences between Calvinism and Lutheranism have developed in history and cannot be properly understood by anyone who is ignorant of the relevant historical factors.

The Calvinist and the Lutheran, to stick with our example, need to participate in one another's history through sympathetic historical understanding. If we are to understand why a segment of the church developed the way it did, we must know what dangers and challenges it faced. To foster genuine ecumenism, Calvinists must study Luther's life and thought, while Lutherans ought to study Calvin in an effort to determine why he felt he had to disagree with Luther on certain points.

VIII

This emphasis on the continuing importance of the doctrinal and confessional traditions within Christianity should not be taken to mean that Christianity renounces any claim to universality or "universalism." Christianity is indeed a universal religion, but what does this mean? A. A. van Ruler writes: "The Israelite and Christian perspective is universalistic: at stake is the brotherhood of all men. But this can only be achieved if all the nations confess the God of Israel."[26]

Submission to Israel's God and to Jesus Christ is the prerequisite for unity. But in the authority that belongs to Christ as King and Lord lies a universality and a possibility for a greater unity than has ever been realized. Christ is not just King of His church. Abraham Kuyper writes: "We misunderstand the kingship of

Christ if we seek it solely in the assembly of the believers. His kingship extends throughout all the world . . ."[27] We may speak of a unity of world history rooted in providence and in Christ's kingship.

The notion of Christ as the center and unifier of history has been transformed and secularized by philosophers, especially Hegelians and Marxists. We must be careful not to confuse Christ's kingship and unification of history with Hegel's "cunning of reason" and immanent eschatology in which the historical process itself brings forth unity and harmony. The vision of Christian universality calls for a different road to the consummation of history. Neither is revolution in the Marxist sense a prerequisite for establishing the Kingdom of God. The Christian instead appeals for reformation and for a submissive obedience to God's will and plan in history.

Christ will unify His people and establish His Kingdom universally—but in His own time and His own way. The challenge in the area of ecumenism is to do what we can to help the process along, through both prayer and action.

CHAPTER TWELVE

INSTITUTIONAL IDENTITY

I

RELIGIOUS intentions and commitments are normally associated with individual human beings: people, it seems, are religious, but cats, rocks, streets, and stars are not. Hence, when we talk about religious rights, prerogatives and freedoms, we are talking about human beings.

This might sound plausible, but it leaves various questions to be answered, questions that arise in connection with such institutions and social structures as churches, schools, and political parties. That churches can have religious intentions and commitments seems reasonable, but what about schools and political parties?

If we find this question difficult to discuss, it is because our thinking about society is largely individualistic. We saw in Chapter 7 that individualism and collectivism are the two dominant social philosophies: pluralism runs a poor third. Collectivism is implicitly totalitarian and tends to make all institutions and organizations branches or parts of the state. Individualism, which is dominant in the Anglo-American political tradition, fights back and defends the rights of the individual, including his freedom of religion.

The Reformation is often taken to be a milestone in the development of individualism because the Reformers successfully defied the wide-ranging authority of the medieval church. The Enlightenment, however, is the era in which individualism was given its classic formulation. The Enlightenment distrust of institutions, which is somewhat understandable given the social and political circumstances of the time, was to have an important impact on the shape of modern society.

Liberal Christianity was deeply influenced by the Enlightenment and therefore developed a conception of religious rights and freedom which emphasized the danger of authoritarianism. The fear was that the integrity and spirituality of the individual would be stifled by oppressive control or by manipulation on the part of institutions. James Hitchcock observes: ". . . the history of modern liberal Christianity has been primarily a flight from everything in religion which is binding and powerful, everything which appears to restrict the full freedom of the individual."[1]

If our social philosophy in effect does not recognize institutions, regarding them as mere collections of individuals, it will have little to say about rights and freedoms for institutions. We see this reflected in how academic freedom is understood. One might suppose that academic freedom belongs to academic institutions, and that it represents their power and right to conduct their affairs in a manner which will, in their judgment, enable them to attain their goals. Not so. In a book on "academic freedom in our time," we read that academic freedom must not be attributed to the governing board, which is the institution in a corporate sense, for the board might then start making decisions about what is to be taught and how it is to be taught: "The academy is free when the scholars who make it are free, as scholars. And the academy is free when its governing board is free to protect and to advance this freedom."[2] Likewise, in a book on academic freedom and tenure we are told: "Academic freedom is that freedom of members of the academic community, assembled in colleges and universities, which underlies the effective performance of their functions of teaching, learning, practice of the arts, and research."[3]

This individualistic conception and use of academic freedom has led to protests in our time, some of them from Christians. Robert C. Sproul complains that academic freedom has become a "shibboleth" and argues: ". . . this freedom cannot extend to the point of *autonomy* if the purposes of a confessional institution are to be served. Yet it now seems to be considered an inalienable right of professors to teach whatever they want."[4]

The individualism underlying our conception of rights and freedoms poses a problem for Christians, who must ask themselves whether our system of laws will allow Christian institutions to remain true to their commitment and identity. Does freedom of religion apply to institutions? What happens when a Protestant theology professor teaching in a Protestant institution converts to

Catholicism? May the institution dismiss him as no longer suitable for the task for which he was appointed? Or could the professor claim that such a dismissal would amount to religious discrimination against Catholics? How would a case of this type be dealt with in the courts? And what happens when children of a Christian family become orphans and wards of the state? May the state place them in an atheistic environment, or must it respect the wishes of the deceased parents that the children be raised as Christians?

II

Although most Christian educators claim to favor academic freedom in some form or another, their secular counterparts often argue that there can be no genuine academic freedom in a confessional or denominational college or university.[5] Any "dogmatic" or "authoritarian" teaching is incompatible with academic freedom and the spirit of scientific inquiry. Charles William Eliot, who was president of Harvard University for forty years, maintained that the word *education* is "a standing protest against dogmatic education":

> Philosophical subjects should never be taught with authority. They are not established sciences; they are full of disputed matters, open questions, and bottomless speculations. It is not the function of the teacher to settle philosophical and political controversies for the pupil, or even to recommend to him any one set of opinions as better than any other. Exposition, not imposition, of opinions is the professor's part.[6]

What Eliot calls "dogmatic" teaching is often referred to as *indoctrination.* This word has taken on some unpleasant connotations in our time and is therefore avoided by many people who do favor education in which authority plays an important role, education in which students are asked to accept certain ideas because some authority can be adduced to vouch for them. Sidney Hook sees relatively little place for indoctrination in a free society:

> Indoctrination is the deliberate use of non-rational means, or the dishonest use of irrational means, to induce beliefs. The second kind of indoctrination is never justified, and the first only in the early years before the powers of intelligence have been awakened. Any kind of indoctrination on the high school or college level is a violation of the integrity of the student's person, or of his right to his own personal growth.[7]

There are even *Christians* who object strongly to specifically Christian education in the sense of an attempt to persuade students of the correctness of Christian doctrine, dismissing any such effort as "authoritarian."[8]

Almost all Christian educational institutions reject neutrality: they want to "teach Christianity" to their students. Their goal is to encourage Christian thinking and conduct. But to pursue this goal they must themselves be committed. How can a school be committed?

The commitment of a school is much like that of a church or denomination. In other words, some sort of statement of basis and purpose is essential. The purpose is to offer Christian education of a specific sort, and the basis officially adopted spells out what the school takes the term *Christian* to mean. Some schools speak of the statement of basic principles as an "educational creed." Various others use creeds which churches have adopted as doctrinal standards, such as the Westminster Confession and the Heidelberg Catechism.

It is sometimes argued that church creeds are inappropriate for schools because they deal with church matters. This argument misrepresents the great creeds of Christendom, for the creeds deal primarily with human life in its totality and only secondarily with specific ecclesiastical functions such as the administration of the sacraments. The major creeds certainly can serve to spell out a school's vision of the Christian life. On the other hand, it would be helpful if a school could include in its statement of basic principles what it takes education to be. Creedal statements, as we saw earlier, should not be too detailed and should not seek to rule on every issue; yet an "educational creed" surely ought to include some specific affirmations about education. The historic creeds of Christendom may have to be supplemented when used in a school setting. As for a statement of basic principles to be used by a Christian political party, it would need supplementary material regarding the political order.

III

If a Christian educational institution defines its objectives by means of a creed, exclusion of some sort will undoubtedly be called for, an exclusion of ideas and perhaps also of certain people who hold them. The creed is supposed to direct the school: everything that goes on educationally ought to be in harmony with it. This raises the issue of toleration once again. The argument is often heard that Christians, of all people, should be models of tolerance.

John Locke, who has deeply influenced both Christians and non-Christians on this subject, argued that toleration is "the chief characteristic mark of the true church." Like John Stuart Mill two centuries later, Locke was convinced that the truth could survive without protection: ". . . the truth certainly would do well enough if she were once left to shift for herself."[9]

Many believers involved in the governance of Christian educational institutions do not believe this is the case. They point to the secularizing of numerous Christian institutions and argue to the contrary that error does indeed drive out the truth. Therefore they insist on holding Christian schools and the teachers and professors who offer instruction within them to the identity officially adopted.

Christian institutions, like individual believers, have to struggle to remain faithful to their commitments and goals. In the process the toes of teaching personnel are sometimes stepped on. What sorts of measures are appropriate when dealing with teachers, professors and preachers who stray from the creedal basis of the school or church they serve? Thomas Oden, reflecting on this question as it arises in the church, maintains: ". . . there can and must be no punishment for heterodox teaching other than simply withholding of the religious body's approval or permission to preach. That cannot be an offense against a civil right, because the ordination to preach is not a civil right."[10]

Oden's position is not a popular one in our tolerant, pluralistic society. Yet it is essentially what John Locke prescribed. The church, which he characterized as a "free and voluntary society," has the right to expel wayward members after first subjecting them to exhortation and admonition:

> If by these means the offenders will not be reclaimed, and the erroneous convinced, there remains nothing further to be done but that such stubborn and obstinate persons, who give no ground to hope for their reformation, should be cast out and separated from the society. This is the last and utmost force of ecclesiastical authority. No other punishment can thereby be inflicted, than that, the relation ceasing

between the body and the member which is cut off, the person so condemned ceases to be part of that church.[11]

IV

Many Christians are uneasy about excommunication, the deposition of clergymen, and the removal of professors from teaching offices. To be sure such disciplinary measures are not pleasant. One good reason for the uneasiness about discipline is that those whose teaching and preaching are regarded as incompatible with the commitments of the institution are sometimes mistreated. Our age is very sensitive to the mistreatment of individuals by institutions.

Edward Schillebeeckx and Hans Küng, two controversial Roman Catholic theologians against whom the Church has taken certain measures, draw a good deal of attention and sympathy for just this reason. Schillebeeckx has made it known that he believes his human rights are not being respected.[12] This is surely a matter of concern: Christian churches should be models of fairness.

The question of fairness also comes up in connection with the way people who are expelled or excommunicated are treated in certain Anabaptist and Mennonite circles, where it is maintained that the offender must be "shunned." The Dordrecht Confession of Faith (1632), which serves some Mennonite churches as a doctrinal standard, declares:

> . . . if any one—whether it be through a wicked life or perverse doctrine—is so far fallen as to be separated from God, and consequently rebuked by, and expelled from, the church, he must also, according to the doctrine of Christ and His apostles, be shunned and avoided by all the members of the church (particularly by those to whom his misdeeds are known), whether it be in eating or drinking, or other such like social matters. In short, that we are to have nothing to do with him; so that we may not become defiled by intercourse with him, and partakers of his sins; but that he may be made ashamed, be affected in his mind, convinced in his conscience, and thereby induced to mend his ways.[13]

The Confession states that the person being shunned must not be treated as an enemy: the excommunication is for his own good and is intended to lead him to repentance. In some circles, however, shunning was carried so far that it was ruled that a believer is to have no sexual relations with an excommunicated spouse. Thus the practice of excommunication does sometimes lead to unfair treatment. Even the courts have gotten involved on occasion.

V

Conflicts in churches and Christian educational institutions are not always about personnel and appointments. To the extent that democratic decision-making is encouraged, there will inevitably be disagreement and a certain amount of skirmishing. We see nothing strange about the notion of political maneuvering in the nation's capital, but somehow we want to keep "politics" out of the church and Christian educational institutions. Declarations of unity often mask what is really going on.

The Catholic theologian Karl Rahner, who argues that we must think in terms of "free speech" in the church, maintains: "If there is, as there should be, a real public opinion within the Church, not merely an unthinking reflection of the Church's official views, a certain tension is likely to exist around all those matters that are subject to change and hence to free discussion."[14]

The tension has increased considerably in the Roman Catholic Church since Rahner wrote these words. The Second Vatican Council (1962-65) led progressives to anticipate major changes. There were indeed changes, but they were less sweeping than the progressives had hoped for and expected. The result was a growing political dissatisfaction within Catholicism: the structures of the church were denounced as authoritarian and then increasingly ignored.

Rosemary Ruether speaks of an unofficial "existential schism" that has taken place within Catholicism. She writes: "Spiritually we are already in schism."[15] There is a deep rift between the Catholic academy and the church hierarchy, she claims. What is needed is "the equivalent of the French Revolution in the Church, the deposing of a monarchical for a democratic constitution of the Church." Since this cannot be expected to happen, the progressives will have to promote pluralism in order to give themselves room to operate: "This means not just theological but ecclesiastical pluralism in the Church—in effect, an internal schism."[16]

This is frightening language, and the danger is by no means confined to Catholicism. "Ecclesiastical pluralism" and "internal schism" are also taking hold in Protestant denominations. Clearly, politics and decision-making within the church need our careful consideration: we must not take it for granted that everything will go smoothly. Churches must ask themselves whether the system of church government they are using is adequate to our time.

Fear of fragmentation should not lead us to discourage all dissent and "political" activity within the church. There are responsible ways to go about these things, as Karl Rahner explains. Borrowing a comparison from British parliamentary democracy, he calls for "loyal" opposition and argues that ". . . there are circumstances in which people can have a real duty to speak their minds within the permitted limits and in a proper spirit of respect, even though this will not bring them praise and gratitude 'from above' (how many examples there are of this in the history of the saints!)." Rahner warns that the church must not create the impression ". . . that she is of the same order as those totalitarian states for whom outward power and sterile, silent obedience are everything and love and freedom nothing . . ."[17] In the church as in the state, power may not be regarded as an end in itself.

VI

In our individualistic age, those who are out to reform or change the church sometimes use tactics that should not meet with our approval. When we contend for the faith, the end does not justify the means. In earlier eras, however, it was especially the institution, the church, that violated this principle. In its eagerness to maintain its identity and position of power, the church treated dissenters and heretics and rebels in ways of which we are ashamed today.

Augustine, who served as a bishop in the North African city of Hippo, helped to formulate the rationale for the harsh treatment of heretics. What it came down to is that the church knows better, just as a mother knows better than her impetuous two-year-old child who wants to play on the busy street in front of the house. Those who go wrong sometimes have to be restrained in their error—if only for the sake of others whom they might mislead. Augustine eventually came to the conclusion that *the state* should take action against heretics.

The darkest episode in the mistreatment of heretics was the

medieval Inquisition. The Inquisition was established by Pope Gregory IX in 1231 to keep political considerations out of the picture as much as possible when the charge of heresy was raised. Yet there was a good deal of corruption among the inquisitors, to say nothing of the cruelty first in the investigation and then in the punishment of convicted heretics. If the punishment was execution, it was carried out by the state. The Inquisition was active mainly in certain parts of Europe where the threat of heresy and rebellion was great; later it was used against witches.

Mistreatment of heretics was by no means limited to Catholicism. Perhaps the most famous heretic ever to be executed was Michael Servetus, who was burned at the stake in Calvinist Geneva in 1553 because of his rejection of the doctrine of the Trinity. Calvin agreed that Servetus ought to die, but he urged a less painful mode of execution.

Servetus was only one of hundreds of heretics and Anabaptists executed by Protestant authorities. Yet his case has come to symbolize a flaw in the thinking of the Reformers. Calvinism paid dearly for this mistake, which has exposed it to much scorn and harsh criticism over the years. Hendrik Van Loon, for example, writes:

> For now it was shown, and shown with brutal clearness, that those Protestants who had clamored so loudly and persistently for "the right to their own opinions" were merely Catholics in disguise, that they were just as narrow-minded and cruel to those who did not share their own views as their enemies and that they were only waiting for the opportunity to establish a reign of terror of their own.[18]

The Servetus story should not be swept under the carpet; the mistake must be frankly admitted. Thomas Oden writes: ". . . anyone who risks digging up the thorny question of heresy must be willing to learn from the chequered history of its abuse. To make good on this commitment, Christians today must be willing to work as hard as anyone to preserve political toleration for unpopular religious views."[19]

VII

We must not act superior, however, as we look back at Christian forbears who took strong measures against heretics. Even though their actions are not ultimately excusable, they are certainly understandable to some extent. Remember that Paul advised: "As for a man who is factious [Greek: *hairetikon*], after admonishing him once or twice, have nothing more to do with him, knowing that such a person is perverted and sinful; he is self-condemned" (Titus 3:10-11). Elsewhere he warned against "party spirit" (Greek: *haireseis*) as one of the "works of the flesh" and added: "I warn you, as I warned you before, that those who do such things shall not inherit the kingdom of God" (Galatians 5:19-21).

Heresy, then, was long taken to be not just sinful but downright dangerous. In the Middle Ages it was sometimes compared to disease: public health measures were called for. Heresy was not simply disagreement but dissension, rebellion, a threat to society. Carey McWilliams writes: "The basis of heresy has always consisted in *a challenge to the existing order*."[20]

The heretics—or some of them, at least—made such nuisances of themselves that something had to be done, but by whom? The church and the state, instead of dealing with the question of tolerance separately, mixed and confused their roles. The church began to determine who the disturbers of the peace were and then either punished them herself or turned them over to the state to be dealt with. No proper separation of the functions of church and state, which is the key to solving the problem of tolerance, had been worked out.

Absolute tolerance was—and is—out of the question. The church today is sometimes compelled to remove a person from a teaching or preaching office, and the state cannot tolerate conspiracy to subvert the political process and replace it with a dictatorship or foreign rule. Even academic freedom has certain limits. The philosopher Arthur Lovejoy, who helped to formulate the modern conception of academic freedom, argued that since members of the Communist Party are committed to overthrowing academic freedom, they should not be allowed to hold teaching positions.[21]

VIII

Yet to be considered is another major reason why the church must be very careful not to get carried away in its campaign against the threat posed by heretics. The Thirty-Nine Articles of the Church of England affirm that even though "sometimes the evil have chief authority in the Ministration of the Word and Sacraments," God's grace and His message to us come through. If we receive the sacraments in faith, they will ". . . be effectual, because of Christ's institution and promise, although they be ministered by evil men."[22] A baby baptized by a heretic or a hypocrite need not be rebaptized.

The stand taken here in the Thirty-Nine Articles goes back to a controversy in Augustine's lifetime. One of the heresies Augustine faced was Donatism, the view that the sacraments are not valid if administered by an unworthy priest. Augustine's response to this view brought out the centrality and sovereignty of divine grace, which was a point he loved to emphasize. God could work even through a heretic! Augustine maintained that the sacrament is valid unless the *recipient* is spiritually unprepared; purity is not required in the priest. Here we think of the high priest Joshua in Zechariah's vision standing before the angel of the Lord "clothed with filthy garments" (see Zechariah 3).

Heresy, then, is a threat to the institutional identity and commitment of Christian churches and schools, but the heretic's capabilities are not to be overestimated. God remains sovereign: the purposes of His grace will be fulfilled despite the heretic—and perhaps even through him!

CHAPTER THIRTEEN

DOCTRINAL AND ACADEMIC FREEDOM

I

MUCH of our society is animated by an ancient faith—the commitment to reason. And reason takes on concrete form in science. Some critics complain that science has gotten modern man into serious difficulty with regard to the pollution of the environment, to take one problem as an example. The usual response is that if science has created the problem, it will also have to solve it. After all, where else could we look for a solution?

If science is to be effective, it must be free. Intellectual freedom or freedom of thought, freedom to form one's own views, is widely regarded as fundamental to the progress that has been made in the Western world. Where science is fettered, as in the Communist world, there are fewer scientific and technological breakthroughs.

The plea for intellectual freedom goes back a long way in history. The poet John Milton cried: "Give me the liberty to know, to utter, and to argue freely according to conscience, above all liberties."[1] Today we hear eloquent, impassioned defenses of academic freedom.

What is academic freedom? Arthur Lovejoy, one of the thinkers responsible for the development of the American conception of academic freedom, defined it as follows:

> Academic freedom is the freedom of the teacher or research workers in higher institutions of learning to investigate and discuss the problems of his science and to express his conclusions, whether through publication or in the instruction of students, without interference from political or ecclesiastical authority, or from the administrative officials of the institution in which he is employed, unless his methods are found by qualified bodies of his own profession to be clearly incompetent or contrary to professional ethics.[2]

In upholding academic freedom we are protecting the university, which is a very special institution in our society. Henry Steele Commager characterizes it as a "citadel of reason" and "the least corrupt institution in American life." He compares the university to the church, for it is ". . . the one institution that associates us with the past and the future, the one institution that has, through all of our history, served, or tried to serve, the interests of the whole of mankind or the interests of truth."[3] The university is also a shining symbol of hope for Robert MacIver. He tells us that part of the university's legacy is "the substitution of reason for passion in the treatment of controversial issues."[4] The Greek distrust of feeling, emotion and passion (see p. 40 above) lives on in our universities.

II

Does such a conception of the university leave room for a *Christian* university in which confessional commitments play a directing role in scholarship? MacIver answers this question with a firm *no*, arguing that a Christian basis would lead to a "total perversion" of the function of the university. "To make the university a center for the propagation of any creed, of any system of values that divides group from group, is to destroy the special quality and the unique mission of the university as a center for the free pursuit of knowledge wherever it may lead."[5] Walter Metzger defends the same point of view and uncovers the ultimately religious significance of science and the university in our culture:

> . . . academic freedom has come to signify the brotherhood of man in science that is akin in aspiration to the brotherhood of man in God. Attempts to foist upon the academic community an American or a Presbyterian science, or a class or color yardstick in appointments and promotions, are thus infringements of academic freedom. By acquiring the value of neutrality, academic freedom has come to stand for the belief that science must transcend ideology, that professors must renounce all commitments that corrupt the passion for truth.[6]

Christians today are too quick to agree with such claims. It is true that some academic institutions have been held back because of closed-mindedness on the part of Christian trustees and administrators, whether Presbyterian or Lutheran or Catholic. Yet this should not lead us to completely renounce the notion of a directing role for faith or revelation in science. However many misconceptions there may be, however many short-cuts Christians may have tried to take in the past, the question of a Christian science remains open. There is still much to be said on the subject.

III

Severe critics of Christianity claim that religious commitments leave no room for genuine scientific and scholarly work. They argue that consequently there can be no such thing as free, living Christian theology. For the Christian everything is cut-and-dried; all the issues were settled centuries ago. If anything genuinely new is proposed, it is automatically branded heresy.

Such a line of argument misrepresents Christianity, to say the least, for there is exegetical, doctrinal and theological freedom within the Christian tradition. Theologians recognize that various passages in Scripture seem to be open to two or more conflicting interpretations, and so they disagree openly with one another. Moreover, Bible study is never purely an attempt to get at a meaning formulated thousands of years ago: an application to our time is sought. Dorothee Sölle therefore calls for "existential interpretation" of Scripture, arguing that ". . . there is no such thing as faith untranslated."[7]

This notion of "translation" is important for the work of the church, for preaching and evangelizing. W. H. Velema observes: "For the sake of our own youth and those who are outside the church, we will indeed have to 'translate' the Biblical message. Translating does not mean transforming but interpreting in a clear, contemporary manner."[8]

Okke Jager adds a word of caution, however. We may not simply throw out the Bible's comparisons and examples as we "translate." They are and remain part of the Biblical message:

> In the concrete thinking of the Old Testament, "The Lord is my shepherd" is a reality that can be verbally expressed only in this manner. To help modern man understand Psalm 23, we must make it clear to him through television documentaries, through exegesis and through catechetical instruction what a shepherd was in that time and that land. Anyone who regards this as too much trouble can simply write off Psalm 23.
>
> We will have to continue to use the images of the Old Testament

> right to the end of time, for it pleased God to reveal Himself in concrete historical situations. Even in the age of the robots, the Lord is my shepherd.[9]

The modern mind, then, does not become a norm by which the Biblical message is to be reshaped or repackaged. In fact, contemporary man needs to relearn some of that Old Testament "concrete thinking."

IV

There is not just exegetical freedom in the church; there is also doctrinal and theological freedom. Many Christians tend to overestimate the danger of free theological discussion. Abraham Kuyper, however, in a lengthy work devoted to the nature of theology, argued that the theologian—as theologian—should not feel too constricted by the church's confessional stance. Kuyper maintained that the theologian is called to render a distinct service to the church by the exercise of his freedom:

> . . . in the service of the Holy Spirit, theology is called ever and anon to test the historic, confessional life of the Church by its source, and to this end to examine it after the norm of the Holy Scripture. By itself confessional life tends to petrify and to fall asleep, and it is theology that keeps the Church awake; that lends its aid in times of conflict with oft-recurring heresies; that rouses her self-consciousness anew to a giving of account, and in this way averts the danger of petrification.[10]

Kuyper, of course, distinguished theology, as a scientific or scholarly activity, from doctrine or dogma or confession. Theology has undergone a slow growth and will never be complete: ". . . as a science it can never be at a standstill, but will always advance without ever being able to reach completion."[11]

Kuyper's conception of the freedom of the theologian in relation to the church's confession is significant. The theologian must respect the confession as clothed with the authority of the church: he ". . . should not undervalue the confession of his Church, as if in it a mere opinion presented itself to him over against which, if equal if not with better right, he might place *his* opinion."[12] The theologian must take the confession very seriously, but he must also test it against Scripture as the ultimate norm. In this regard he serves the church.

Kuyper's emphasis on freedom must not be misunderstood.

Theology is free from the church in that it is not essentially an ecclesiastical activity; it has a character and integrity of its own. But for Kuyper this did *not* mean that a theological professor is free to do as he pleases: Kuyper was also very conscious of the right of an institution or organization to stick to a course to which it had committed itself. Thus he wrote:

> That a Church should forbid a minister of the Word the further use of her pulpit when he antagonizes her confession, or that a board of trustees should dismiss a professor, who, according to their view, does not serve the end for which he was appointed, has nothing whatever to do with this *liberty of studies.* A ship-owner, who dismisses a captain because he sails the ship to a different point of destination from what the ship-owner designated, in no wise violates thereby the personal rights of the captain.
>
> The persistent heretic must be banished from the Church; a professor, whose presence is a menace to the highest interests of a school, must be dismissed; but from the field of theology no one can disappear, unless he leaves it of his own free will.[13]

V

Protestantism can speak of doctrinal freedom because its confessions and creeds are historical documents and are therefore recognized as fallible and subject to the Word of God, the unnormed norm. Veneration for the creeds is sometimes carried too far in Protestant circles, but the best Protestant thinkers have always known how to subordinate the creeds to Scripture. The creeds have an important pedagogical function in that they help and guide believers in their reading of Scripture. Yet, even though they shed light on Scripture, in the final analysis they are to be judged and corrected by Scripture. The pedagogical priority they enjoy for many believers does not make them ultimately authoritative.

For Protestantism there is no ultimate authority other than the Word of God. This emphasis is sometimes summed up by means of a phrase used by Paul Tillich—"the Protestant principle." All of the church's creeds, practices, statements, and actions are subject to judgment. "The Protestant principle," writes Tillich, "implies a judgment about the human situation, namely, that it is basically distorted." It is a "permanent criterion of everything temporal." Just as Luther and the original "protesters" opposed the Catholic majority, the Protestant principle ". . . contains the divine and human protest against any absolute claim made for a relative reality, even if this claim is made by a Protestant church. The Protestant principle is the judge of every religious and cultural reality, including the religion and culture which calls itself 'Protestant.' "[14]

Calvinism has long expressed this same point by means of the familiar statement that the work of reformation is never finished: a reformed church is always a reform*ing* church. That's why her theologians must be free to look critically at her confessions and creeds, as Kuyper observed. And changes are sometimes made in the confessions: they are not absolute but are subject to the constant test of God's Word. The Belgic Confession, which serves as a doctrinal standard in various Reformed churches, originally stated that it is the task of the government to ". . . remove and prevent all idolatry and false worship, that the kingdom of antichrist may thus be destroyed and the kingdom of Christ promoted." In the twentieth century various churches concluded that this conception of the government's task is unbiblical, even though it has long been part of the confession, and therefore removed these words from the article on government.[15] The creed was corrected!

VI

Although in principle Christianity supports and demands doctrinal freedom, there have been serious clashes between the doctrines of the church and the findings of science. The most famous case is the Roman Catholic Church's condemnation of Galileo (1564-1642) for defending the heliocentric conception of the universe. When the ecclesiastical officials were done with their investigation of Galileo, they condemned him for holding ". . . the doctrine which is false and contrary to the Sacred and Divine scriptures, that the sun is the center of the world and does not move from east to west and that the earth moves and is not the center of the world."[16]

There has been a good deal of discussion of this puzzling and painful controversy. Jerome J. Langford concludes his book on the subject by observing: "The mistakes made on both sides in

Galileo's conflict with authority have much to teach us. It is obvious that we still have much to learn."[17] Hans Küng regards the treatment meted out to Galileo as a catastrophe of the first magnitude:

> Galileo's condemnation and the consequent loss of the world of science has not unjustly been ranked with the East-West schism and the Western divisions in faith as one of the three greatest disasters in Church history. It played an essential part in opening that gap between the Church and modern civilization which is still far from being bridged.[18]

It is certainly doubtful whether the proper lesson has been learned. Centuries afterward Christians continued to take one or another simple-minded approach to the question of science and religion. Some still subordinated science to theology, thereby stripping the non-theological scholar of his academic freedom, and his discipline of its integrity. Others went much too far in the opposite direction, assuring us that there could not be a conflict between Christian teaching and the results served up by science, for both were seeking God's truth. Daniel Coit Gilman, the first president of the Johns Hopkins University, the university that led the way in the development of graduate education in the United States, took the latter approach, arguing: "Religion claims to interpret the word of God, and science to reveal the laws of God. The interpreters may blunder, but truths are immutable, eternal, and never in conflict."[19] For Gilman, religion thus had nothing to fear from science and the university. But his university, like so many other prominent institutions founded and led by Christians, became secular. There was more to the question of academic freedom and the relation of science to religion than Gilman realized.

VII

Both Christians and secular Humanists claim to be in favor of academic freedom, even if they do not define such freedom in the same way. Yet there is some overlap in meaning. When Fritz Machlup speaks of "the toleration of honest error" as the "essence of intellectual freedom,"[20] both the Christian and the secular Humanist can agree: there must be room for honest error if science is to progress.

To spell out what academic freedom is and is not, certain distinctions must be made; otherwise misconceptions will linger on. Academic freedom might be misconstrued as a form of freedom of speech. Not long after its founding, the University of Chicago, another leader in the development of graduate-level education, declared: ". . . the principle of complete freedom of speech of all subjects has from the beginning been regarded as fundamental in the University of Chicago . . ." This principle, the University went on to state, was never to be called into question.[21]

Is academic freedom then some sort of civil right? Is it the right of every professor to say whatever he pleases as he instructs his students? This would hardly be an adequate conception or definition, for we cannot ascribe academic freedom to every citizen. Sidney Hook argues:

> One of the most widespread myths about academic freedom is that it is a human right or at least entailed by the rights enumerated in "the Bill of Rights" of the Amendments to the American Constitution. This is a gross mistake. However human rights or civil rights be defined, they belong to individuals in virtue of their participation in the human community or as citizens of the democratic commonwealth. They do not have to be earned. Everyone has a human right to a fair trial or to freedom of speech. But not everyone has a right to academic freedom. That must be *earned*. It is only the person who is professionally qualified in some sense who is eligible for academic freedom.[22]

To grasp Hook's point, we must make a clear distinction between the state on the one hand and the university or academy on the other. We can speak of academic freedom only in relation to the academy; no such freedom is granted or guaranteed by the state. And academic freedom is not freedom of opinion. Not even the most liberal university would allow a physics professor to teach students utterly absurd ideas about the physical structure of the universe.

Earlier we saw that a clear distinction must be made between the church and the state if the question of tolerance is to be dealt with properly. The state is obliged to tolerate things that a church need not tolerate. A Presbyterian church, for example, might depose or dismiss a clergyman for holding Catholic views, but it would be improper for the state to take any sort of action against him. The state would be obliged to ignore his doctrinal differences with Presbyterianism, whereas the church could take no other action against him than to remove him from office and conceivably from its fellowship altogether.

To deal with the academic freedom question, we must distinguish the church and state contexts from one another and then from the school context. The Christian ideal of academic freedom means freedom from both church and state control. This was the idea behind the founding of the Free University of Amsterdam in 1880, and the same principle has led to the rise of a system of North American Christian day schools that are free from both church and state.

VIII

What are the main outlines of a Christian conception of academic freedom? This question can be handled in three points, by distinguishing between the academic freedom of educational institutions, of professors, and of students.

First of all, Christian educational institutions enjoy academic freedom in that they are not—or should not be—controlled by either the state or the church. A church may operate a theological seminary for the training of pastors or an institution for training lay workers of various sorts, but full-fledged Christian scholarly activity ought to be carried on in institutions that concern themselves specifically with education and scholarship and do not subordinate their interests to those of the business world or of government or of the church.

As far as the professors are concerned, there are three points to be made. First, the academic freedom of the professor is his freedom to learn from anyone—not just from approved sources and authorities. Here it is helpful to remember Augustine's comparison with the children of Israel leaving Egypt: they took with them the treasures of the Egyptians which they claimed for themselves "as if to put them to a better use."[23] We should bear in mind, however, that when Christian scholars learn from their secular counterparts, they are not necessarily picking up what secular thinkers might want to teach them. One can learn from bad examples and from mistakes, including the mistakes of others. A great philosopher like Hegel may be fundamentally wrong, but what is important is that he is *profoundly* wrong. There is much more to be learned from him than from a mediocre thinker who is also wrong.

Secondly, the Christian professor, because he teaches at the college level, must be left free in the organization, arrangement and selection of the materials he deals with. The standardization of curriculum common in elementary school is not appropriate at the college or university level. The prerogatives of the professor, as a specialist in the field which he is teaching, must be respected. A board of trustees should not dictate how a philosophy professor is to teach a course in the history of medieval philosophy.

Thirdly, the Christian professor must be left free to develop his own program of research and writing. Inquiries and suggestions are appropriate, but the scholar should determine for himself where his calling lies. All adult believers enjoy the Christian liberty of serving where they believe they have been called. This general principle must not be forgotten when it comes to Christian scholarship: there are many worthwhile projects that could be undertaken, but the scholar must make a choice, a choice for which he is directly responsible to God.

As for the students, finally, there are two aspects to be distinguished in their academic freedom. First, Christian students on the college and university level should share in the shaping and planning of their program of study. Secondly, they are to make up their own minds about theoretical issues. A professor may require of them that they learn and be able to state certain views and theories which he chooses to include in his course, but he may not require them to hold to his own views, or any other set of views, for that matter. A professor who violates this principle encroaches on the student's integrity. Agreement with the professor may never be a requirement for passing a course or receiving a good grade.

IX

Academic freedom is well worth fighting for. Free theology benefits the church, and free science serves life. But we must be careful to keep these connections in mind, or we may wind up regarding freedom as an end in itself, which is what modern Humanism does when it interprets freedom as autonomy, as man's drive for self-actualization. Hans Küng sums up the modern outlook as follows: "Man today is expected to liberate himself. Emancipation as man's self-determination as opposed to authority accepted in blind faith, to unauthorized dominion, is necessary: freedom from natural constraint, social constraint, from the self-constraint of the person who has not come to terms with himself."[24]

The Bible presents us with a rather different perspective and asks us to be willing to subordinate our freedom—including our academic freedom—to others. Our freedom has a purpose. Paul writes: "You were called to feedom, brethren; only do not use your freedom as an opportunity for the flesh, but through love be servants of one another" (Galatians 5:13).

Even this orientation toward the other is not the last word. Our exercise of freedom must be placed in a still wider context. Paul also writes: "So, whether you eat or drink, or whatever you do [academic work is not exempted], do all to the glory of God" (I Corinthians 10:31). This is the same note struck by the Westminster Shorter Catechism, which opens with the question: "What is the chief end of man?" The memorable answer reads: "Man's chief end is to glorify God, and to enjoy him forever."[25]

CHAPTER FOURTEEN

THE PLACE OF APOLOGETICS

I

WHEN we turn to the subject of apologetics, we face a paradoxical situation: this discipline, which is often understood as an effort to justify Christian belief, is itself in need of justification in our time. Apologetics has acquired a bad reputation. Robert Nowell writes that it is now widely regarded as "an unconvincing defence of the indefensible, a rehearsal of plausible excuses for the sins of the Church's past life, a polemical exercise conducted on a fiercely partisan and denominational basis."[1]

Apologetics is widely associated with argument, which sets people apart. Since our age seems to value unity more than certainty, it does not care to hear arguments. Instead of working out ways to deal with disputes, we often ignore them.

There are various considerations underlying the unpopularity of apologetics. Three of them will be dealt with here. The first is that the apologist often gives away or concedes too much. He is like an ambassador who has been posted for too long in a dazzling foreign capital: the time finally comes when the government he represents begins to wonder whose side he is on. The Christian apologist, as an ambassador to the world of science and culture, sometimes seems to switch allegiance and may even wind up defending the inherent goodness of the world of science and culture.

When an ambassador assumes his responsibilities in a foreign capital, he forsakes his own soil and takes up residence outside his country. The role of the apologist is often conceived of in similar terms. Edgar Y. Mullins sums up the task of the defender of Christianity as follows: "It is to establish the Christian position by means of the principles of investigation employed by the opposition, so far as those principles are valid."[2] The defender of the faith moves on to his opponent's turf, as it were; he begins by seeking common ground.

This strategy has been criticized by leading Christian thinkers. In a discussion of the struggle between Christianity and modernism, Abraham Kuyper complains: "In this struggle apologetics have not advanced us one single step. Apologists have invariably begun by abandoning the assailed breastwork . . ."[3] J. Gresham Machen worries about all the concessions that are made: "In trying to remove from Christianity everything that could possibly be objected to in the name of science, by trying to bribe off the enemy by those concessions which the enemy most desires, the apologist has really abandoned what he started out to defend." Machen draws a lesson from this: ". . . the things that are sometimes thought to be hardest to defend are also the things that are most worth defending."[4]

Christian apologists are not the only ones to make this mistake. C. G. Jung, whom Freud branded a "heretic" for deviating from orthodox psychoanalysis (see p. 86 above), also followed the strategy of concession when he was invited to give some lectures in the United States. In a letter he explained his strategy to Freud, who later commented: "Jung boasted . . . that his modifications of psycho-analysis had overcome the resistances of many people who had hitherto refused to have anything to do with it. I replied that that was nothing to boast of, and that the more he sacrificed of the hard-won truths of psycho-analysis the more would he see resistances vanishing."[5] Christian apologists would do well to ponder this exchange between Jung and Freud as they consider how to present the "scandal" of the gospel to an unbelieving world.

Some of the suspicions raised about apologists are justified, but this should not lead us to abandon apologetics altogether. A better conclusion to draw would be that we must be careful in how we defend the gospel. Should ground be given up? Robert Knudsen declares simply: "One ought to defend the Christian faith without taking a position outside of that faith."[6]

II

A second reason for the bad reputation of apologetics is that various people regard it as intellectually dishonest. The famous definition of metaphysics as "the finding of bad reasons for what we believe upon instinct"[7] could also be applied to apologetics, which might then be regarded as a lawyer's brief aimed more at persuasion than at truth.

Many of the pluralist defenses of Christianity fall into this category. If pluralism turns out to be a gentle relativism, how can it serve as a justification of the Christian faith? I can well understand why people sometimes regard the pluralist rhetoric uttered by Christians as hypocritical or less than honest. As I indicated, the good points being made by way of the language of pluralism can better be formulated in terms of the Christian conception of tolerance in the political sphere.

Dishonest defenses of Christianity can easily lead outsiders to view Christianity as an ideology, and it is indeed characterized as such on occasion.[8] What we call theology is for some opponents of Christianity simply an ideology, a justification and rationalization of the economic, social and political position of dominance achieved by the Western world, and more specifically by certain groups within our society. Ideology, in the ears of many, is an ugly word. Lewis Feuer observes that all ideologies "tend to become authoritarian."[9] Hannah Arendt shows us more of the dark side of ideology when she argues that all ideologies contain "totalitarian elements," even if they are fully developed only by totalitarian movements.[10]

Such objections can be countered to some extent, although they are not entirely without justification. We should take them as a reminder not to slip into intellectual dishonesty when we engage in apologetics, and also as a warning not to make Christian thinking appear to be a rationalization and justification of our economic, social and political position. In the light of the Christian message about human sinfulness, we, too, stand condemned.

III

A third major objection to apologetics is that it is too intellectualistic: it seems to assume that people can be argued into accepting and believing the gospel. Herman Bavinck warns against the "exaggerated expectations" sometimes aroused by apologetics, ". . . as though by reason it could change the heart and through argumentation could cultivate piety."[11] Abraham Kuyper concurs and warns against the "gross error" of viewing reasoning as the foundation (*grondslag*) for faith.[12]

Such an approach would clearly place too much emphasis on rationality and would denigrate other aspects of the life of the mind. G. K. Chesterton argues that reason by itself, with nothing to balance it, easily turns into insanity:

> The madman is not the man who has lost his reason. The madman is the man who has lost everything except his reason.
>
> The madman's explanation of a thing is always complete, and often in a purely rational sense satisfactory. Or, to speak more strictly, the insane explanation, if not conclusive, is at least unanswerable; this may be observed specially in the two or three commonest kinds of madness. If a man says (for instance) that men have a conspiracy against him, you cannot dispute it except by saying that all the men deny that they are conspirators; which is exactly what conspirators would do. His explanation covers the facts as much as yours.[13]

In the face of this overemphasis on reason Chesterton calls us to mysticism: "Mysticism keeps men sane. As long as you have mystery you have health . . ." Mystery even plays an important role in explanation and gaining a proper outlook on life. Chesterton tells us that the secret of mysticism is that ". . . man can understand everything by the help of what he does not understand. The morbid logician seeks to make everything lucid, and succeeds in making everything mysterious. The mystic allows one thing to be mysterious, and everything else becomes lucid."[14] The will of God may be a mystery to us, but we must make it our starting point in understanding this world.

The danger of madness is not the only objection to the excessive emphasis on reason of which many apologists are guilty. A more significant danger is that the rational approach may lead to the erection of a natural theology. Herman Bavinck observes that such a course has been taken by many Protestant thinkers, who sought *proofs* for God's existence and for the truths of divine revelation: "The conviction that the proofs [for God's existence] were sufficient to bring about at least a human faith contributed unwittingly to the emancipation of reason from faith and to the placing of the dogmas of natural theology and of holy Scripture outside saving faith." This led to rationalism in the Protestant churches. The eventual result was:

> Natural theology came to stand alongside revealed theology as independent of it . . . Leibniz was expressing the dominant view when he placed revelation over against reason as an external emissary facing an authorized assembly. This assembly first investigates revelation's letters of faith, and if it finds them genuine it listens respectfully. What deism in England and rationalism in Germany deduced from this before long is that natural theology is completely sufficient.[15]

Such an approach to Christianity is indeed too intellectualistic. Again, we should take the criticism of apologetics as a timely warning. But it is not by itself a reason to forsake the apologetic task.

IV

If there is indeed an apologetic task that remains, what does it consist of? What, exactly, is apologetics? A good place to begin looking for an answer is the Bible. The text that is usually quoted is: "Always be prepared to make a defense to any one who calls you to account for the hope that is in you, yet do it with gentleness and reverence" (I Peter 3:15).

In the light of this text we can say that apologetics, generally speaking, is the explanation and defense of the Christian faith. We might best regard this task as having three separable divisions or aspects within it. Let us look at them one by one.

First of all, the apologist seeks to deal with misapprehensions about Christianity and unjustified charges that might arise. In a history of apologetics we read: "The earliest apologists were primarily concerned with obtaining civil toleration for the Christian community—to prove that Christians were not malefactors deserving the death penalty."[16]

Calvin's *Institutes of the Christian Religion* can also be viewed as an apologetic work in this sense. In Calvin's day Protestants were persecuted and mistreated in many parts of Europe. Wild accusations swirled in the air. Calvin therefore attached to his *Institutes* a "prefatory address" to King Francis I of France in which he declared: ". . . our adversaries cry out that we falsely make the Word of God our pretext, and wickedly corrupt it. By reading our confession you can judge according to your prudence not only how malicious a calumny but also what utter effrontery this is."

Yet this apologetic treatise, like so many others, was not meant for outsiders only: it also proved valuable for instructing believers about Christian doctrine. Calvin had this additional purpose in mind all along.[17]

V

A second aspect of the apologetic task is somewhat neglected nowadays—historical apologetics. There is a battle of ideas going on around us, a battle for men's minds and hearts. Countless books, essays and articles are written for and against the various worldviews and outlooks that compete for our allegiance. This means that a great deal is written about Christianity and its history—much of it false.

We need historical apologetics to set the record straight. Christianity would be well served if fresh accounts of various episodes and aspects of history could be written. We are often told, for example, that Christianity encouraged and called for the exploitation of nature that has given rise to global pollution. This charge represents a misunderstanding of Biblical teaching and Christian history, and therefore needs refutation by a historical apologist.

Augustine's greatest work, *The City of God*, can be read as historical apologetics. Augustine lived in the declining days of the Roman empire, when Christianity was being blamed for many of the ills of the time, especially by Romans who wanted to return to the old paganism. Recognizing the potential for great harm to the Christian cause, Augustine wrote his massive account of the two cities and their history to set the historical record straight.

Professional historians often criticize this kind of history, especially as practiced by Orosius, a protégé of Augustine who wrote a Christian world history in the same vein. Historians appeal for objectivity and claim that the historian must not have an ax to grind, a point he is trying to prove. To the extent that they are right in appealing for objectivity—and their account of objectivity might well be called into question—we could answer this charge by distinguishing clearly between historical science as such and historical apologetics. The Christian historian should indeed strive for fairness and impartiality when he undertakes to write the history of a certain country or period. What this means, in effect, is that he must not approach the research phase of his work with his conclusions already formulated, although he may well have a working hypothesis in mind. But this does not mean that a Christian historian may not also serve on occasion as a historical apologist. He might choose, for example, to write a biography of John Calvin with the express purpose of refuting some of the absurd accusations made against Calvin.

VI

So far we have distinguished two aspects of the apologetic task. First, the apologist clearly explains Christian teaching in order to clear up misconceptions and thereby win greater toleration for Christians. Secondly, he sets the historical record straight by refuting unjust charges and providing an alternative account of events in which justice is done to the Christian cause. What happened during the Inquisition is clearly indefensible, but it was not quite as wicked and corrupt as some secular historians would have us believe.

The third aspect of the apologetic task is attack on the alternatives to Christianity offered by the modern mind. Various thinkers present Christianity as arbitrary and absurd, while Humanism is completely responsible and unproblematic, involving no hidden presuppositions. If such characterizations of the choice facing man today are not challenged and countered, they will do much harm to the Christian cause.

The Christian thinker most often associated with such an approach to apologetics is Emil Brunner. Peter Vogelsanger explains that apologetics, for Brunner, is "the attack of faith on the strongholds of disbelief." What is attacked, more specifically, is the "natural self-understanding in which man entrenches himself against God's claim."[18] Given the many forms of Humanistic and anti-Christian thinking flourishing in our age, this aspect of the apologetic task represents a very significant project requiring a major infusion of the Christian community's resources.

In various sports it is said that the best defense is a good offense. This is the strategy behind apologetics as critique of modern thinking. Without this kind of response to the modern challenge, Christianity may wind up sounding too defensive. The philosophies of our day must be shown to rest on arbitrary assumptions and choices. Cornelius Van Til has done valuable work in this area.

VII

What does it mean to contend for the faith? Part of the answer, surely, is that we fight for our beliefs by engaging in apologetics. Christians were slow to learn that they are not to use the power of the sword to advance the gospel, but they quickly saw the potential in the power of the pen, and thus it can be said that apologetics is as old as Christianity. The battle in which we are to engage on behalf of the faith is a spiritual battle, and it is fought with spiritual weapons.

Does this battle also rage *inside* the church? Brunner evidently thinks so. We cannot draw a clear line to separate heresy inside the church from disbelief outside the church. Vogelsanger, expounding Brunner, writes: "Just as dogmatic theology is constantly necessary as an encounter of faith with the heresy in the church, apologetics is necessary as a constant encounter with disbelief in the world, and, as disbelief persistently infiltrates from the world, it is also necessary in the church."[19]

Abraham Kuyper used a different name for the kind of theology that does battle for the truth within the church: he called it *polemics*. The task of polemics, he writes, is ". . . to defend the confessed truth over against error, the orthodox confession over against the heterodox one, and to demonstrate the untenability of heresy."[20] Perhaps the term *polemics* can best be reserved for disputes between those who call themselves Christians, while *apologetics* could refer to the encounter of Christianity with explicitly non-Christian ways of thinking.

VIII

This raises the question of the place of apologetics in relation to theology generally. There is one major thinker, Karl Barth, who does not believe that apologetics and theology (or dogmatics) should be separated at all: dogmatics should include the polemic and apologetic task. (His reasons for taking this position are bound up with his discontinuous, existentialistic conception of revelation.) Barth, as dogmatician, has not been afraid to confront the non-Christian thinkers.

Such an issue is hard to settle because there is always something arbitrary about how we use words. For many people today, the term *theology* simply means Christian reflection about everything and anything. When the term is so used, of course, it includes apologetics. But I prefer to use it in a more restricted sense in which we leave room for other branches of Christian thought, other Christian scholarly disciplines. I believe there is a good deal to be said for the definition of theology offered by James Smart: "Theology is the careful systematic investigation of the problem of truth and error in the church's message and principles."[21]

Various Christian thinkers maintain that apologetics or inquiry into "Christian evidences" for God's existence and for the truth of the Bible plays a foundational role with respect to theology: theology is to be erected on the groundwork laid by apologetics. Clark Pinnock, for example, warns against "fideism" and argues: "Faith rests upon an attested and authenticated revelation. The task of apologetics is to ground the truth claim of the gospel."[22] This was also the position of Benjamin B. Warfield, one of the best known of the Princeton Calvinists.

Although Warfield was on friendly terms with Kuyper and Bavinck, these two Dutch Calvinist theologians did not agree with him on this matter. Bavinck argued: "Apologetics cannot precede faith and does not try to prove the truth of revelation a priori."[23] More simply: "Apologetics is the fruit, never the root, of faith."[24]

This is not to say that Bavinck and Kuyper recognized no task for apologetics. The point is simply that they assigned to apologetics and to reason generally a less elevated place than many other Christian thinkers did. A distinction made by John Baillie can help us here: ". . . the clearing away of obstacles, and especially of obstacles which have no right to be there, is a different process from the laying of a sure foundation . . ."[25] Apologetics, to stick with the analogy, is not part of the edifice of theology.

IX

This distinction between theology (or dogmatics) and apologetics can help us deal with a much-misunderstood charge hurled at Christianity. We are sometimes told that Christianity is not so much false as irrelevant: Christian teaching represents a series of answers to questions that modern man no longer asks. If modern man does not know what the questions are, that is, if Christianity's questions are no longer questions for him, how can the answers possibly mean anything to him?

It must be admitted that there is something to this charge: many people today simply do not and cannot understand traditional Christian teaching. But from this admission we should not draw the conclusion that Christian teaching must be changed to meet modern man's "needs." Modern man and his outlook may not become normative for theology; rather, modern man must look to the Bible to find out what his true needs are. There must be a radical change first in his heart and then in his understanding of himself if he is to be able to grasp the meaning of Christian teaching and the gospel. It may be that modern man is not now able to grasp Christian teaching, but he can *become* able—by the route of submission and self-denial.

This does not mean, however, that Christianity should turn a deaf ear to the request for a "relevant" presentation of Christian teaching and the gospel. Apologetics, precisely because it is not a part of theology, can play a valuable mediating role here. Thus apologetics can and should include a "presentation of the gospel for our time" in which a special effort is made to counter the objections that arise from the mentality dominant today.

This is essentially to say that apologetics is time-bound to a much greater extent than theology and Christian teaching as laid down in the creeds and confessions. Apologetics must change as the predominant outlook changes. Thus James Orr observes that ". . . every age calls for an apologetic suited to itself."[26] The apologetics of a C. S. Lewis or a G. K. Chesterton is especially effective for certain kinds of people, for these two Christian writers each addressed a specific type of mind. Adept as these apologists are in explaining the faith and removing needless barriers to belief, their writings will not be effective in all times and situations, just as the work of Christian analytic philosophers is of rather limited usefulness. There is no end to the apologetic task. Thus no one need complain that there is never anything new in apologetics.

X

The successful Christian apologist will draw considerably on the work of theologians; indeed, many apologists are themselves theologians. But the apologist will need more than theology to make his case: he will also require the help of Christian philosophers, for the latter are especially equipped to provide him with insight into the structure of the modern mind.

There is a tendency in some Christian circles to equate apologetics with Christian philosophy, in part because various apologists are philosophers. This is a mistake, for a number of reasons. For one thing, part of the apologetic task falls outside philosophy's usual concerns and is more historical in character. Moreover, a great deal of what philosophers (and therefore also Christian philosophers) occupy themselves with has no direct bearing on apologetics, even if it turns out to be relevant in a secondary sense. Christian philosophy is independent of both theology and apologetics and should have a place of its own in Christian academic institutions. Christian answers are needed to the questions which philosophers ask.

For comparable reasons, we should not equate apologetics with philosophy of religion either, although the overlap is much greater in this case. There is nothing wrong with asking a philosopher of religion to teach apologetics, perhaps in a theological seminary, but philosophy of religion should be recognized as a philosophical discipline with an agenda or list of topics of its own, an agenda that is relatively fixed and permanent, whereas apologetics, as I indicated, tends to change with the times.

Apologetics, then, is not a carefully circumscribed scholarly discipline that can be given its own limited place in the academic world. Apologetics is the task of the Christian community collectively, for it is part of the work of Christian witness, of presenting the gospel to the unbelieving world. Some Christians are much more effective in this work than others, but it should be the concern of all of us, so that God's name may be glorified.

POSTSCRIPT

DO IDEAS MAKE A DIFFERENCE?

I

THE discussion of heresy and apologetics might yet prove to be entirely "academic" in the sense of irrelevant. If a certain notion accepted by many modern thinkers turns out to be true, we would have to conclude that there is no need to oppose heresy or to try to bring people around to a different point of view through apologetics. That notion is the belief that ideas make no difference to human life, conduct and action. It is money that makes the world go around—or perhaps love, or sex. Ideas have nothing to do with it.

In his book on heresy Barrows Dunham speaks of the conviction of the English that "thinkers are not dangerous, even in dissent."[1] If this were true, a policy of the broadest possible toleration would seem to be called for, also in the church. But is it true? Many thinkers believe it is. Sidney Hook observes: "Some thinkers have denied that ideas are ever relevant to action . . ." This would seem to suggest that ". . . fanatics, no matter what ideas they are fanatical about, are entitled to the same opportunities, other things being equal, as anyone else."[2]

Hook does not agree but rather holds out for the significance of ideas. His is the traditional view that was aptly expressed by the English biologist Thomas Henry Huxley, who spoke at the Johns Hopkins University in 1876, the year the university opened, and declared that "men live not by bread, but by ideas."[3]

Orthodox Christians, of course, are inclined to side with Huxley; otherwise their emphasis on doctrine becomes pointless. Yet the more recent conception of ideas and their place in human life deserves some consideration. If we are to contend for the faith in the sense of fighting for Christian ideas and ideals, we must be able to defend our conviction that ideas make a difference in human life.

II

Those who question the relevance and importance of ideas are not contesting their reality. What is at issue is priority. Do ideas come before actions? Are actions to be understood as consequences of prior ideas? Or are ideas perhaps caused by actions? Are they mere reflections of actions?

This issue can be clarified by a comparison with a conception of the emotions developed by William James and sometimes also attributed to the Danish philosopher C. G. Lange. This theory can be stated as follows: ". . . our experience of emotion is really our experience of the bodily changes 'following on the perception of an exciting fact', so that it is nearer the truth to say that we are afraid because we run away than that we run away because we are afraid."[4] James himself explained it in these words:

> Common-sense says, we lose our fortune, are sorry and weep; we meet a bear, are frightened and run; we are insulted by a rival, are angry and strike. The hypothesis here to be defended says that this order of sequence is incorrect, that the one mental state is not immediately induced by the other, that the bodily manifestations must first be interposed between, and that the more rational statement is that we feel sorry because we cry, angry because we strike, afraid because we tremble, and not that we cry, strike, or tremble, because we are sorry, angry, or fearful, as the case may be.[5]

Ideas, like emotions, are sometimes said to follow—rather than precede and cause—actions. The sociologists of knowledge have worked out all sorts of variations on this theme. One of the sources from which they draw inspiration, of course, is Karl Marx. In *The German Ideology*, which was written jointly by Marx and Friedrich Engels, we find the famous statement: "Life is not determined by consciousness, but consciousness by life."[6]

This notion has undergone some refinement at the hands of later theorists of "ideology," but the main thrust still comes through in the work of many philosophers and social scientists today. Ideas are not to be taken at face value, for they represent false consciousness or rationalization. D.J. Manning neatly sums up the original conception as follows: "According to Marx and

Engels an ideology is a systematic attempt to demonstrate the rationality of the existing distribution of wealth and the social utility of the order in which the wealthy hold positions of power. It is invariably an apology for institutionalized inequality."[7]

In this conception of ideology we see a convergence of Marxism and pragmatism. Ideas are caused by life or action, but they do have a certain instrumental value: they serve as tools enabling us to get and hold what we want. Truth is subordinated to utility. Ideas or ideologies arise out of the situations in which people find themselves, but they also help them alter and transform those situations.

III

When we transfer all of this to the domain of Christian thinking, the primacy of praxis (i.e. action, life) over theory (i.e. thinking, ideas) becomes an emphasis on orthopraxis as opposed to orthodoxy (see pp. 107-10 above). In short, we face the notion of Christianity as essentially a way of life rather than a set of teachings or doctrines. The Bible and Christian doctrine, we are told, spring from Christian living and represent a record in which Christian praxis is reflected.

There are definite dangers in this way of thinking, which tends to push aside a Christian confessional unity in favor of what we might call "Christian ethnicity." Christians are then people who happen to have inherited a certain way of life, a heritage which they continue to cherish. Since we live in a "pluralistic society" (not a melting pot in which differences are gradually eliminated but a cultural mosaic in which differences are cherished and encouraged), Christians should cling to their way of life as a valuable component of our society, which would be poorer without it. And this brings us back to pluralist rhetoric as a "cheap defense" of the Christian faith: our Christian ideas or doctrines are mere reflections of our way of life and ought to be tolerated and even encouraged since they are essentially harmless. The underlying assumption, of course, is that ideas ultimately make no difference.

IV

It is significant that the Communist totalitarian countries, which pose such a threat to peace, do not accept this pluralist rhetoric and the gentle relativism underlying it. As far as the Communist countries are concerned, ideas *do* make a difference. Dissenters often wind up in psychiatric hospitals where they are subjected to drug treatments designed to weaken their mental integrity. Or they may be sent to special camps for political re-education. Building on the work of the Russian physiologist Ivan Pavlov, the political police have even ventured into "brainwashing."

Brainwashing was much talked about in the 1950s and early 1960s, but it is not a popular topic today. Many people in our time would rather denounce smaller, less powerful countries like South Africa than face up to the barbarous inhumanity of the Soviet Union. The novelty of having Aleksandr Solzhenitsyn in our midst has worn off.

When brainwashing was still a lively concern, the psychiatrist Joost Meerloo coined the word *menticide* to describe this full-scale assault on the human mind, this weakening and destruction of the human personality: "Menticide is an attack on man's very mind, on his sovereign will and conviction. It destroys free thought and makes servile, mechanical instruments of his inviolate thought processes."[8] In a compelling book entitled *The Rape of the Mind*, Meerloo appealed for "inner backbone," "mental backbone," and "mental integrity."[9] He called on the United Nations to take measures against menticide and "psychological intrusion," which is a violation of "a human right as precious as physical existence, the right of the nonconforming free individual—the right to dissent, the right to be oneself."[10]

Meerloo uses strong language here: he speaks of a "right to be oneself." Is he perhaps going too far? Can't I remain the person I am even if my ideas have been changed through brainwashing and "psychological intrusion"? Is there really such a thing as menticide?

If we take the term *ideas* in the abstract, theoretical sense, we might be inclined to respond that I can remain the person I am even though my ideas have been forcibly changed or destroyed. But if my ideas are the Christian teachings I adhere to, my Christian confession and commitments, the answer must be *no*. I argued earlier that a Christian is not essentially his deeds or his conduct but what he is striving to become as he puts his sins and failures behind him (see pp. 110-11). In a real sense, the Christian *is* his beliefs, his convictions, his commitments. Therefore Meerloo is right to speak of brainwashing as a form of killing, just as we could speak of killing if a dissenter was subjected to surgery that brought his brain activity to an end while allowing his bodily functions to continue.

Totalitarian powers know perfectly well that ideas make a difference. Therefore they engage not just in brainwashing but in a control of all schools, a control that is designed to bring independent thinking to an end. The purpose is not so much to make everyone enthusiastic about the official totalitarian ideology as to destroy the very capacity to form independent convictions.

The ability to maintain one's convictions in the face of enormous pressure has stood Christians in good stead over the centuries. There have been martyrs in all centuries; ours is no exception. We, too, may be pressured to deny Christ, or to make of Him something less than what He revealed Himself to be. That was the pressure faced by Polycarp, who was a second-century battler for orthodoxy and an opponent of Gnosticism, which he denounced as a "satanic falsification of the truth." Just before he was put to death, Polycarp declared: "Eighty-and-six years I have been in the service of Christ, and He has never done me wrong; how, then, can I blaspheme Him now,—my King and my Savior?"[11]

NOTES

INTRODUCTION

1. See Thomas Oden, *Agenda for Theology* (San Francisco: Harper and Row, 1979), pp. 102, 95.

2. *"Fundamentalism" and the Word of God* (Grand Rapids: Eerdmans, 1958), p. 177.

3. Roland Bainton, *Here I Stand: A Life of Martin Luther* (Nashville: Abingdon, 1978 reprint), p. 15.

4. *Battle for the Mind: A Physiology of Conversion and Brainwashing* (Garden City, N.Y.: Doubleday, 1957), p. 146.

5. See Edward A. Dowey, Jr., *A Commentary on the Confession of 1967 and an Introduction to "The Book of Confessions"* (Philadelphia: Westminster Press, 1968), p. 40.

6. *Christian Attitudes Toward War and Peace* (Nashville: Abingdon, 1960), p. 64.

7. *Christian Unity and Christian Diversity* (Philadelphia: Westminster Press, 1975), pp. 10, 109.

8. "Instruction on Excommunication," in *The Complete Writings of Menno Simons,* trans. Leonard Verduin and ed. John C. Wenger (Scottdale, Pennsylvania: Herald Press, 1956), p. 962.

9. See "A Kind Admonition on Church Discipline," in *Complete Writings,* p. 413, and "A Clear Account of Excommunication," in *Complete Writings*, p. 483.

10. "Christian Scholarship and the Defence of the Faith," in *What Is Christianity?* (Grand Rapids: Eerdmans, 1951), p. 130.

11. Avery Dulles, *A History of Apologetics* (New York: Corpus, 1971), p. 1.

CHAPTER 1: DEFINING THE FAITH INDUCTIVELY

1. *The Church Trap* (New York: Macmillan, 1968), p. 21.

2. *Protestant-Catholic-Jew: An Essay in American Religious Sociology,* revised edition (Garden City, N.Y.: Anchor Books, 1960), p. 84; see also p. 258.

3. "America's Civil Religion: What It Is and Whence It Came," in *American Civil Religion*, ed. Russell E. Richey and Donald G. Jones (New York, Evanston, San Francisco, and London: Harper and Row, 1974), pp. 77-8).

4. *Outlines of a Philosophy of Religion Based on Psychology and History* (New York: Harper and Brothers, 1957), p. 131.

5. "The Proclamation of the Gospel in a Pluralistic World," in *The Proclamation of the Gospel in a Pluralistic World: Essays on Christianity and Culture* (Philadelphia: Fortress Press, 1973), p. 11.

6. *The Faith of Modernism* (New York: Macmillan, 1925), p. 13.

7. *New Faith for Old: An Autobiography* (New York: Macmillan, 1936), p. 106.

8. "The Essence of Christianity," in *God and the Universe of Faiths: Essays in the Philosophy of Religion* (London: Macmillan, 1973), p. 119.

9. *Catholicism and Modernity: Confrontation or Capitulation?* (New York: Seabury Press, 1979), p. 224.

10. *Alice in Wonderland* and *Through the Looking-Glass* (New York: Grosset & Dunlap, no date), p. 216.

11. Will Herberg, "The Strangeness of Faith," in *Faith Enacted as History* (Philadelphia: Westminster Press, 1976), p. 77.

12. "Mission and Humanization," in *Mission Trends No. 1: Crucial Issues in Mission Today,* ed. Gerald H. Anderson and Thomas F. Stransky (New York: Paulist Press; and Grand Rapids: Eerdmans, 1974), p. 240.

13. *Christian Unity and Christian Diversity* (Introduction, note 7), pp. 24-5.

14. "Church Outside the Church," in *The Truth Is Concrete,* trans. Dinah Livingstone (New York: Herder and Herder, 1969), pp. 103, 105, 106.

15. *On Being a Christian,* trans. Edward Quinn (Garden City, N.Y.: Doubleday, 1976), pp. 27-8.

16. See "Het wezen des Christendoms," in *Verzamelde opstellen op het gebied van godsdienst en wetenschap* (Kampen: J. H. Kok, 1921), p. 24.

17. See II Corinthians 11:12-13.

CHAPTER 2: DEFINING THE FAITH IN HISTORY

1. Paul Tillich, *A History of Christian Thought: From Its Judaic and Hellenistic Origins to Existentialism*, ed. Carl E. Braaten (New York: Simon and Schuster, 1968), pp. 33-4.

2. See *The Mission and Expansion of Christianity in the First Three Centuries,* trans. and ed. James Moffatt (New York: Harper and Brothers, 1962, reprint of the 1908 edition), p. 314.

3. *Outlines of the History of Dogma*, trans. Edwin Knox Mitchell

(Boston: Beacon Press, 1957, reprint of the 1893 edition), pp. 58-9.

4. *Progress of Dogma* (Old Tappan, N.J.: Fleming H. Revell Company, no date), p. 55.

5. "Het wezen des Christendoms" (Ch. 1, n. 16), p. 29.

6. *Christelijke wetenschap* (Kampen: J. H. Kok, 1904), p. 88.

7. *The Philosophy of Revelation* (Grand Rapids: Eerdmans, 1953), p. 227; see also p. 309.

8. Translation taken from *Creeds of the Churches,* revised edition, ed. John H. Leith (Atlanta: John Knox Press, 1973), p. 31.

9. See *Orthodoxy* (Garden City, N. Y.: Image Books, 1959, first published in 1908), pp. 100-1.

10. "Creed or Chaos?" in *The Whimsical Christian* (New York: Macmillan, 1978, first published in 1969 as *Christian Letters to a Post-Christian World*), p. 41.

11. "The Essence of Christianity," in *God and the Universe of Faiths* (Ch. 1, n. 8), pp. 113-14.

12. "The Development of the Concept of 'Orthodoxy' in Early Christianity," in *Current Issues in Biblical and Patristic Interpretation: Studies in Honor of Merrill C. Tenney Presented by His Former Students,* ed. Gerald F. Hawthorne (Grand Rapids: Eerdmans, 1975), p. 47.

13. "Dogma," in *A Handbook of Christian Theology: Definition Essays on Concepts and Movements of Thought in Contemporary Protestantism,* ed. Marvin Halverson and Arthur A. Cohen (New York: New American Library, 1958), p. 80.

14. Translation taken from J. N. D. Kelly, *The Athanasian Creed* (London: Adam and Charles Black, 1964), pp. 17-20.

15. *Agenda for Theology* (Introduction, n. 1), pp. 86-7.

16. *An Autobiography* (London: Oxford University Press, 1939), p. 31.

CHAPTER 3: REVELATION AND REASON

1. *Reason and Life,* trans. Kenneth S. Reid and Edward Sarmiento (New Haven: Yale University Press, 1956), p. 157.

2. *The Theology of the Early Greek Philosophers* (London, Oxford and New York: Oxford University Press, 1967), p. 48.

3. *The Theology of the Early Greek Philosophers,* p. 164.

4. *The Greeks and the Irrational* (Berkeley and Los Angeles: University of California Press, 1968), p. 218.

5. *The Greeks and the Irrational,* p. 185.

6. See Henri and H. A. Frankfort, "The Emancipation of Thought from Myth," in *Before Philosophy: The Intellectual Adventures of Ancient Man,* by Henri and H. A. Frankfort et al. (Baltimore: Penguin Books, 1949), p. 262.

7. *Existentialism and Religious Liberalism* (Boston: Beacon Press, 1962), pp. 59-60.

8. *The Interpretation of Religion* (New York and Nashville: Abingdon Press, no date), p. 75.

9. *Varieties of Christian Apologetics* (Grand Rapids: Baker Book House, 1962), p. 22.

10. *Varieties of Christian Apologetics*, p. 95.

11. Quoted by David Cairns, "Natural Theology," in *A Handbook of Christian Theology* (Ch. 2, n. 13), p. 251.

12. "Conscience in a Pluralistic Society," in *Ecumenical Dialogue at Harvard: The Roman Catholic-Protestant Colloquium,* ed. Samuel H. Miller and G. Ernest Wright (Cambridge: Harvard University Press, 1964), pp. 226-7.

13. *Neoplatonism of the Italian Renaissance* (London: George Allen & Unwin, 1935), p. 63.

14. Quoted by William J. Wolf, "Anglicanism and Its Spirit," in *The Spirit of Anglicanism*, ed. William J. Wolf (Wilton, Connecticut: Morehouse-Barlow, 1979), p. 144.

15. See his *Essay Concerning Human Understanding*, 2 volumes (New York: Dover Publications, 1959), Book IV, Chapter 19, pp. 428ff of Vol. II. On reason see especially p. 433.

16. *Controversy: The Humanist/Christian Encounter* (London: Pemberton Books, 1971), p. 82.

17. *Christianity Not Mysterious* (Stuttgart and Bad Cannstatt: Friedrich Frommann Verlag, 1964, reprint of the 1696 edition), p. 146.

18. *Christianity Not Mysterious,* p. 20, italics omitted.

19. *Christianity Not Mysterious,* pp. 34-5.

20. See Ramm, *Varieties of Christian Apologetics,* pp. 113, 123-4.

21. *On Being a Christian* (Ch. 1, n. 15), p. 31.

22. *Marx Against the Marxists: The Christian Humanism of Karl Marx,* trans. John Drury (Maryknoll, N.Y.: Orbis Books, 1980), p. xi.

23. Moses Hadas, *Humanism: The Greek Ideal and Its Survival* (New York: Harper and Brothers, 1960), p. 123.

24. *Controversy*, p. 228.

25. *Conversations with Luther: Selections from the Recently Published Sources of the Table Talk,* ed. Preserved Smith and Herbert Percival Gallinger (New Canaan, Connecticut: Keats Publishing, 1979), p. 115.

26. "Instruction on Excommunication" (Introduction, n. 8), p. 961.

27. *"Fundamentalism" and the Word of God* (Introduction, n. 2), pp. 138, 161; see also p. 139.

28. *Athens and Jerusalem*, trans. Bernard Martin (New York: Simon and Schuster, 1968), p. 255.

29. *Athens and Jerusalem,* pp. 280-1.

30. *Athens and Jerusalem,* p. 282.

31. *Athens and Jerusalem,* p. 288.

32. *Athens and Jerusalem,* p. 398.

33. *Critique: Its Nature and Function,* trans. Henry J. Koren (Pittsburgh: Duquesne University Press, 1967), pp. 152-3.

34. *A Treatise of Human Nature,* ed. L. A. Selby-Bigge (Oxford: Clarendon Press, 1888), Part III, Book 2, Section 3, p. 415.

35. *Concerning Scandals,* trans. John W. Fraser (Grand Rapids: Eerdmans, 1978), p. 12.

CHAPTER 4: REVELATION AND EXPERIENCE

1. *On Religion: Addresses in Response to Its Cultured Despisers,* trans. Terrence N. Tice (Richmond: John Knox Press, 1969), pp. 141-2.

2. *Philosophie und Theologie bei Schleiermacher* (Zollikon and Zurich: Evangelischer Verlag, 1947), pp. 124-5.

3. See *The Idea of the Holy: An Inquiry into the Non-Rational Factor in the Idea of the Divine and Its Relation to the Rational,* trans. John W. Harvey (New York: Oxford University Press, 1958), pp. 144, 145-6, 143.

4. *E Voto Dordraceno: Toelichting op den Heidelbergschen Catechismus* (Amsterdam: J. A. Wormser, 1892-95), Vol. III, p. 596.

5. "St. Paul's Use of the Argument from Experience," in *Selected Shorter Writings of Benjamin B. Warfield*, ed. John E. Meeter (Nutley, N.J.: Presbyterian and Reformed Publishing Company, 1970-73), Vol. II, p. 150.

6. *The Prescriptions Against the Heretics,* in *Classic Statements on Faith and Reason,* ed. E. L. Miller (New York: Random House, 1970), p. 5.

7. " 'Nature' as Norm in Tertullian," in *Essays in the History of Ideas* (New York: Capricorn Books, 1960), p. 315.

8. *Institutes of the Christian Religion*, 2 vols., trans. Ford Lewis Battles and ed. John T. McNeill (Philadelphia: Westminster Press, 1960), 1.3.1.

9. *Institutes,* 1.5.1.

10. See *Christian Faith: An Introduction to the Study of the Faith,* trans. Sierd Woudstra (Grand Rapids: Eerdmans, 1979), pp. 48-9.

11. See the Third and Fourth Heads of Doctrine, Article 4.

12. *Our Reasonable Faith,* trans. Henry Zylstra (Grand Rapids: Baker Book House, 1977, reprint of the 1956 edition), p. 59.

13. *The Philosophy of Revelation* (Ch. 2, n. 7), p. 28.

14. See *Biblical Theology: Old and New Testaments* (Grand Rapids: Eerdmans, 1948), pp. 31-2, 37ff.

15. *Christian Faith,* p. 48.

16. *Institutes,* 4.14.18.

17. *Religion and the Christian Faith* (Philadelphia: Westminster Press, no date, first published in 1956), pp. 347, 342.

18. *Christian Faith*, p. 75.

19. "The Barmen Declaration," in *Creeds of the Churches* (Ch. 2, n. 8), p. 520.

20. *Reformed Dogmatics* (Grand Rapids: Reformed Free Publishing Association, 1966), p. 19.

21. "Heresy and Concession," in *Selected Shorter Writings,* Vol. II, p. 677.

CHAPTER 5: SCRIPTURE AS REVELATION

1. *The Faith of Modernism* (Ch. 1, n. 6), pp. 54, 50.

2. See "The Modern Use of the Bible," in *What Is Christianity?* (Introduction, n. 10), pp. 193, 196.

3. *"Fundamentalism" and the Word of God* (Introduction, n. 2), p. 153.

4. "Inerrancy in Current Debate," in *Beyond the Battle for the Bible* (Westchester, Illinois: Cornerstone Books, 1980), p. 50.

5. See Harold Lindsell, *The Battle for the Bible* (Grand Rapids: Zondervan, 1976).

6. "Inerrancy in Current Debate," p. 38.

7. *The Faith of Modernism,* p. 47.

8. See Donald E. Miller, *The Case for Liberal Christianity* (San Francisco: Harper and Row, 1981), p. 15.

9. *Confessions of a Conservative Evangelical* (Philadelphia: Westminster Press, 1974), p. 99.

10. I believe that in a significant sense the Bible is indeed a history book: see my book *Reading the Bible as History* (Burlington, Ontario: G. R. Welch, 1980), especially Chapters 1-3.

11. *What Is Faith?* (Grand Rapids: Eerdmans, 1946), p. 241.

12. Article 6; the "Chicago Statement" is reproduced in *Inerrancy,* ed. Norman Geisler (Grand Rapids: Zondervan, 1979), see p. 495.

13. See Jack Rogers and Donald McKim, *The Authority and Interpretation of the Bible: An Historical Approach* (San Francisco: Harper and Row, 1979), pp. 274ff.

14. *Systematic Theology* (Grand Rapids: Eerdmans, 1979 reprint), Vol. I, p. 170.

15. I, x; see *Creeds of the Churches* (Ch. 2, n. 8), p. 196.

16. *On Being a Christian* (Ch. 1, n. 15), p. 81.

17. See Bonhoeffer's *Letters and Papers from Prison,* revised edition, ed. Eberhard Bethge (New York: Macmillan, 1967), pp. 144, 171-2.

18. See G. C. Berkouwer, *A Half Century of Theology,* trans. and

ed. Lewis B. Smedes (Grand Rapids: Eerdmans, 1977), p. 141.

19. *Shaken Foundations: Theological Foundations for Missions* (Grand Rapids: Zondervan, 1972), p. 2.

20. *Institutes* (Ch. 4, n. 8), 3.23.2.

CHAPTER 6: HISTORY AND TRADITION

1. "Areopagitica," in *Areopagitica and Other Prose Works* (London: J. M. Dent & Sons; and New York: E. P. Dutton & Co., 1927), p. 27.

2. "What Is Enlightenment?" in *The Philosophy of Kant: Immanuel Kant's Moral and Political Writings,* ed. Carl J. Friedrich (New York: Modern Library, 1949), pp. 132-3.

3. "What Is Enlightenment?" p. 132.

4. *Infallible? An Inquiry,* trans. Edward Quinn (Garden City, N.Y.: Doubleday), p. 210.

5. *God, Man, and the Thinker: Philosophies of Religion* (New York: Delta Books, 1962), p. 300.

6. *The Spirit of Protestantism* (London, Oxford and New York: Oxford University Press, 1961), see pp. 171ff.

7. *The History of Skepticism from Erasmus to Spinoza,* revised edition (Berkeley, Los Angeles and London: University of California Press, 1979), p. 4; see also p. 16.

8. *Tradition: Old and New* (Grand Rapids: Zondervan, 1970), p. 74.

9. *Progress of Dogma* (Ch. 2, n. 4), p. 15.

10. *"Fundamentalism" and the Word of God* (Introduction, n. 2), p. 92.

11. *Orthodoxy* (Ch. 2, n. 9), pp. 47-8.

12. *Black Theology and Black Power* (New York: Seabury Press, 1969), pp. 120, 121.

13. "A Black Man's View of Authority," in *Erosion of Authority,* ed. Clyde L. Manschreck (Nashville and New York: Abingdon Press, 1971), p. 91; see also *Black Christian Nationalism: New Directions for the Black Church* (New York: William Morrow & Company, 1972), pp. xvii-xix, xxxv-xxxvii.

14. "Beyond Eve and Mary," in *New Theology No. 9,* ed. Martin E. Marty and Dean G. Peerman (New York: Macmillan; and London: Collier-Macmillan, 1972), pp. 209, 225.

15. On this question see Henry Vander Goot, "*Tota Scriptura:* The Old Testament in the Christian Faith and Tradition," in *Life Is Religion: Essays in Honor of H. Evan Runner,* ed. Henry Vander Goot (St. Catharines, Ontario: Paideia Press, 1981), pp. 97-117.

16. *The Spirit of Protestantism,* p. 216.

17. *The Spirit of Protestantism,* p. 215.

18. "Is 'Scripture Alone' the Essence of Christianity?" in *Biblical*

Authority, ed. Jack Rogers (Waco, Texas: Word Books, 1977), p. 119.

19. See *Infallible?*, pp. 181ff; see also *The Church—Maintained in Truth: A Theological Meditation,* trans. Edward Quinn (New York: Seabury Press, 1980).

20. *The Infallibility Debate,* ed. John J. Kirvan (New York, Paramus and Toronto: Paulist Press, 1971), p. 88.

21. *The Two Horizons: New Testament Hermeneutics and Philosophical Description with Special Reference to Heidegger, Bultmann, Gadamer, and Wittgenstein* (Grand Rapids: Eerdmans, 1980), p. 314.

CHAPTER 7: PLURALISM AND DIVERSITY

1. "The Bible as Realistic Narrative," in *Consensus in Theology? A Dialogue with Hans Küng and Edward Schillebeeckx,* ed. Leonard Swidler (Philadelphia: Westminster Press, 1980), pp. 84, 81.

2. *"Fundamentalism" and the Word of God* (Introduction, n. 2), pp. 18, 19.

3. *The Enlightenment: An Interpretation,* Vol. I: *The Rise of Modern Paganism* (New York: Alfred A. Knopf, 1967), p. 163.

4. *Protestant Faith and Religious Liberty: The Basis of Religious Freedom in Protestant Theology* (Nashville and New York: Abingdon Press, 1967), p. 54.

5. "The Proclamation of the Gospel," (Ch. 1, n. 5), p. 2.

6. *Protestant-Catholic-Jew* (Ch. 1, n. 2), p. 85.

7. *The New Polytheism* (New York, Evanston, San Francisco, and London: Harper and Row, 1974), pp. 60, 27, 4, 28.

8. On this meaning of the term *pluralism,* see *Society, State, and Schools: A Case for Structural and Confessional Pluralism,* by Rockne McCarthy, Donald Oppewal, Walfred Peterson, and Gordon Spykman (Grand Rapids: Eerdmans, 1981), especially pp. 51ff.

9. "Structural pluralism" is the term used in *Society, State, and Schools* (see note 8 above).

10. Matthew L. Lamb, *History, Method and Theology: A Dialectical Comparison of Wilhelm Dilthey's Critique of Historical Reason and Bernard Lonergan's Methodology* (Missoula, Montana: Scholar's Press, 1978), p. xiii.

11. "The Encounter Between East and West in the Civilization of Our Time," in *The Ecumenical Era in Church and Society: A Symposium in Honor of John A. Mackay,* ed. Edward J. Jurji (New York: Macmillan, 1959), p. 98.

12. See "Religious Liberty and the Parable of the Tares," in *Early and Medieval Christianity* (Boston: Beacon Press, 1962), pp. 95, 106-7, 112-13.

13. *Call to Mission* (Philadelphia: Westminster Press, 1970), p. 9.

14. "The Good Fight of Faith," in *God Transcendent and Other Selected Sermons* (Grand Rapids: Eerdmans, 1949), p. 122.

15. *A Letter Concerning Toleration,* ed. Mario Montuori (The Hague: Martinus Nijhoff, 1963), pp. 15, 33.

16. "Particular Questions Within General Consensus," in *Consensus in Theology?*, p. 35.

17. *Catholicism and Modernity* (Ch. 1, n. 9), pp. 110, 85.

CHAPTER 8: THEORY AND DISAGREEMENT

1. *Spinoza and the Rise of Liberalism* (Boston: Beacon Press, 1958), p. 11.

2. See Paul J. Stern, *C. G. Jung: The Haunted Prophet* (New York: George Braziller, 1976), p. 105.

3. "An Autobiographical Study," trans. James Strachey, in *The Standard Edition of the Complete Psychological Works of Sigmund Freud* (London: Hogarth Press and the Institute of Psycho-Analysis), Vol. XX (1959), p. 53.

4. *The Life and Work of Sigmund Freud,* Vol. II (New York: Basic Books, 1955), p. 142.

5. "On the History of the Psycho-Analytic Movement," in *The Standard Edition,* Vol. XIV (1957), p. 43.

6. "On the History of the Psycho-Analytic Movement," p. 49.

7. See *The Study of Theology,* trans. Duane A. Priebe (Philadelphia: Fortress Press, 1978), pp. 2ff.

8. *Progress of Dogma* (Ch. 2. n. 4), pp. 12-13.

9. *Reformed Dogmatics* (Ch. 4, n. 20), p. 4.

10. *The Christian Creeds: A Faith to Live By* (Dayton, Ohio: Pflaum/Standard, 1973), p. 19.

11. *Gereformeerde Dogmatiek* (Kampen: J. H. Kok, 1928-30), Vol. II, p. 458.

12. "Christian Theology: Its Nature and Scope," in *What Theologians Do,* ed. F. G. Healey (Grand Rapids: Eerdmans, 1971), pp. 20, 26.

13. See Deuteronomy 13:1-5; Jeremiah 28:5-9; Galatians 1:6-9; see also G. C. Aalders, *De valsche profetie in Israël* (Wageningen: J. Zomer Drukkerij "Vada," 1911), pp. 180-2.

14. *On Being a Christian* (Ch. 1, n. 15), pp. 446, 448, 581-2.

15. *Does God Exist? An Answer for Today,* trans. Edward Quinn (Garden City, N.Y.: Doubleday, 1980), p. 115.

16. *A History of Western Morals* (New York: Harcourt, Brace and Company, 1959), p. 414.

17. See Anthony Thiselton, *The Two Horizons* (Ch. 6, n. 21), pp. 304ff.

18. See *Agenda for Theology* (Introduction, n. 1), pp. 4-6, 37-40, 49-53, 56, 60-2, 116, 149, 158.

19. *Agenda for Theology*, pp. xii, 122.

20. Quoted by Ernest R. Sandeen in *The Roots of Fundamentalism: British and American Millenarianism, 1800-1930* (Chicago: University of Chicago Press, 1970), p. 115.

21. Quoted by Rogers and McKim, *The Authority and Interpretation of the Bible* (Ch. 5, n. 13), p. 276.

22. See *Systematic Theology* (Ch. 5, n. 14), Vol. I, p. 15.

23. *Van de voleinding,* Vol. I (Kampen: J. H. Kok, 1929), p. 137.

24. *Introduction to Theology: An Invitation to Reflection on the Christian Mythos* (Philadelphia: Fortress Press, 1976), pp. 177, 176.

CHAPTER 9: HERESY AND APOSTASY

1. "The 'Death of God' Theology—And the Living God of the Bible," in *Faith Enacted as History* (Ch. 1, n. 11), pp. 170-1.

2. "The Nature of Heresy," in *Storm over Ethics,* by John C. Bennett et al. (Philadelphia: United Church Press, 1967), p. 130.

3. *The Heretical Imperative: Contemporary Possibilities of Religious Affirmation* (Garden City, N.Y.: Anchor Press / Doubleday, 1979), pp. 30-1.

4. *Heresies* (Garden City, N.Y.: Anchor Books, 1976), pp. 10, 1.

5. *The Faith of Modernism* (Ch. 1, n. 6), p. 64.

6. *Heroes and Heretics: A Political History of Western Thought* (New York: Alfred A. Knopf, 1964), p. 51.

7. Walter Nigg, *The Heretics,* ed. and trans. Richard and Clara Winston (New York: Alfred A. Knopf, 1962), p. 411.

8. *American Religious Heretics: Formal and Informal Trials,* ed. George A. Shriver (Nashville and New York: Abingdon Press, 1966), p. 15.

9. *Heroes and Heretics,* p. 5.

10. See my book *Learning to Live with Evil* (Burlington, Ontario: G. R. Welch; and Grand Rapids: Eerdmans, 1982), Chapter 5.

11. *The Heretics,* pp. 8, 11, 409.

12. *The Spirit of Protestantism* (Ch. 6, n. 6), p. 128.

13. *Heresy, Yes—Conspiracy, No* (Westport, Connecticut: Greenwood Press, 1973), pp. 21, 69, 70 (italicized in original).

14. See *The Church,* trans. Ray and Rosaleen Ockenden (London: Burns and Oates, 1968), pp. 248-9, 257; see also *The Church—Maintained in Truth* (Ch. 6, n. 19), pp. 30-1.

15. Quoted by Malcolm Lambert, *Medieval Heresy: Popular*

Movements from Bogomil to Hus (New York: Holmes & Meier, 1977), p. 4.

16. *Conversations with Luther* (Ch. 3, n. 25), pp. 206-7.

17. *Concerning Scandals* (Ch. 3, n. 35), p. 66.

18. *Utopia: The Perennial Heresy* (New York: Sheed and Ward, 1967), pp. 20-1.

19. *E Voto Dordraceno* (Ch. 4, n. 4), Vol. III, p. 606.

20. Gordon Leff, *Heresy in the Later Middle Ages: The Relation of Heterodoxy to Dissent, c. 1250—c. 1450*, Vol. I (Manchester: Manchester University Press, 1967), pp. 1-2.

21. *"Fundamentalism" and the Word of God* (Introduction, n. 2), p. 44.

22. "Heresy and Concession," in *Selected Shorter Writings* (Ch. 4, n. 5), Vol. II, p. 679.

23. *The Case for Orthodox Theology* (Philadelphia: Westminster Press, 1959), p. 13 (italicized in original).

24. *The Bible, the Church and the Reason: The Three Great Fountains of Divine Authority* (New York: Charles Scribner's Sons, 1892), p. 37.

25. *The Prescriptions Against the Heretics* (Ch. 4, n. 6), pp. 3-4.

26. See "Heresy and Concession," pp. 677-9.

27. See *De valsche profetie in Israël* (Ch. 8, n. 13), pp. 54, 58-61, 181.

28. *No Other Name: The Choice Between Syncretism and Christian Universalism* (London: SCM Press, 1963), pp. 90, 89.

29. See J. A. E. Vermaat, *Christus of ideologie? Positie en keuze van kerken en christenen in een ideologische situatie* (Utrecht: Uitgeverij "De Banier," 1977), pp. 6-7, 11-12, 16-17.

30. *The Living of These Days: An Autobiography* (New York: Harper and Brothers, 1956), pp. 245, 244.

31. *Agenda for Theology* (Introduction, n. 1), pp. 22, 24, 29.

32. "Secularism," in *A Handbook of Christian Theology* (Ch. 2, n. 13), p. 340.

CHAPTER 10: CONFESSIONAL UNITY

1. *Freedom in the Church* (Dayton, Ohio: Pflaum Press, 1969), p. 131.

2. Quoted from the back section of the *Psalter Hymnal* (Grand Rapids: Publication Committee of the Christian Reformed Church, 1959), p. 23.

3. See William J. Wolf, "Anglicanism and Its Spirit" (Ch. 3, n. 14), p. 165.

4. W. H. van de Pol, *Anglicanism in Ecumenical Perspective* (Pitts-

burgh: Duquesne University Press, 1965), p. 26.

5. *Anglicanism,* fourth edition (New York: Oxford University Press, 1978), pp. 387, 254.

6. "Anglicans and the Anglican Vocation," in *Essays in Anglican Self-Criticism,* ed. D. M. Paton (London: SCM Press, 1958), p. 223.

7. *Modern Heresies* (Greenwich, Connecticut: Seabury Press, 1961), p. 162.

8. *The Integrity of Anglicanism* (New York: Seabury Press, 1978), p. 18.

9. *The Church—Maintained in Truth* (Ch. 6, n. 19), pp. 28-9.

10. *On Being a Christian* (Ch. 1, n. 15), p. 410.

11. *Doing Theology in a Revolutionary Situation* (Philadelphia: Fortress Press, 1975), pp. 72, 90, 81.

12. *New Faith for Old* (Ch. 1, n. 7), pp. 288, 285.

13. *The Faith of Modernism* (Ch. 1, n. 6), p. 178.

14. *What Is Faith?* (Ch. 5, n. 11), pp. 39, 18, 23.

15. *Om en om: Een bundel theologie en geloofsbezinning* (Kampen: J. H. Kok, 1972), p. 50.

16. *Heroes and Heretics* (Ch. 9, n. 6), p. 429.

17. *Lectures on Galatians* (1535), in *Luther's Works,* Vol. 27, ed. Jaroslav Pelikan (Saint Louis: Concordia Publishing House, 1964), pp. 37, 41-2.

18. See *Documents of the Christian Church*, second edition, ed. Henry Bettensen (London, Oxford and New York: Oxford University Press, 1967), p. 201.

19. *Commentaries on the First Twenty Chapters of the Book of the Prophet Ezekiel,* trans. Thomas Myers, Vol. II (Grand Rapids: Eerdmans, 1948), p. 8.

20. *The Certainty of Faith*, trans. Harry der Nederlanden (St. Catharines, Ontario: Paideia Press, 1980), p. 71.

21. *The Interpretation of History* (New York and London: Charles Scribner's Sons, 1936), p. 34.

22. *An Essay on the Development of Christian Doctrine* (Westminster, Maryland: Christian Classics, 1968), pp. 29-30.

23. *Progress of Dogma* (Ch. 2, n. 4), p. 9.

24. *The Myth of Christian Beginnings: History's Impact on Belief* (Garden City, N.Y.: Doubleday, 1971), pp. 160, 21.

25. *Heretics* (New York and London: John Lane, 1906), p. 286.

26. *Catholicism and Modernity* (Ch. 1, n. 9), p. 181.

27. "The Good Fight of Faith" (Ch. 7, n. 14), pp. 152, 151.

28. "The Issue in the Church," in *God Transcendent* (Ch. 7, n. 14), p. 47.

29. *Christianity and Liberalism* (Grand Rapids: Eerdmans, 1923), p. 7.

30. "Problemen in de tolerantie-idee," in *Theologisch werk* (Nijkerk: G. F. Callenbach, 1969-73), Vol. IV, p. 173.

31. See Hendrik Kraemer, *The Christian Message in a Non-Christian World* (Grand Rapids: Kregel Publications, 1956, first published in 1938), p. 208.

32. "Theocratie en tolerantie (1956)," in *Theologisch werk,* Vol. I, p. 215.

CHAPTER 11: THE CHALLENGE OF ECUMENISM

1. *Progress, Coexistence and Intellectual Freedom* (New York: W. W. Norton and Company, 1968), p. 27.

2. See *The Brothers Karamazov,* trans. Constance Garnett, translation revised by Avrahm Yarmolinsky (New York: Heritage Press, 1961), Book V, Chapter 5, pp. 195-6.

3. *The Social Sources of Denominationalism* (Cleveland and New York: Meridian Books, 1957), p. 264.

4. *No Other Name* (Ch. 9, n. 28), p. 86.

5. Quoted by Hendrik Van Loon as the epigraph for his book *Tolerance*, revised edition (New York: Liveright Publishing, 1940).

6. *On Being a Christian* (Ch. 1, n. 15), p. 91; see also *Does God Exist?* (Ch. 8, n. 15), p. 627.

7. "Participation: The Changing Christian Role in Other Cultures," in *Mission Trends No. 2: Evangelization*, ed. Gerald H. Anderson and Thomas F. Stransky (New York: Paulist Press; and Grand Rapids: Eerdmans, 1975), p. 229.

8. On this Old Testament syncretism, see M. B. Van 't Veer, *My God Is Yahweh: Elijah and Ahab in an Age of Apostasy,* trans. Theodore Plantinga (St. Catharines, Ontario: Paideia Press, 1980), pp. 35ff, 209ff.

9. *No Other Name,* p. 89.

10. *The Validity of the Christian Mission* (New York, Evanston, San Francisco, and London: Harper and Row, 1972). p. 36.

11. *The Christian Message in a Non-Christian World* (Ch. 10, n. 31), pp. 146, 134-5.

12. *The Christian Message,* p. 119.

13. "The Christian in a Religiously Plural World," in *Christianity and Other Religions,* ed. John Hick and Brian Hebblethwaite (Philadelphia: Fortress Press, 1980), pp. 104-5, 91, 98.

14. *The Problems of Theology* (Cambridge: Cambridge University Press, 1980), p. 150.

15. *A History of Apologetics* (Introduction, n. 11), p. 30.

16. *Stromata,* in *Classic Statements on Faith and Reason* (Ch. 4, n. 6), p. 13.

17. *On Being a Christian,* p. 113.

18. *The Christian Message,* pp. 329, 332.

19. "Proclaiming the Inner Christ of Hinduism: An Interview with Paul Sudhakar," in *Mission Trends No. 5: Faith Meets Faith,* ed. Gerald H. Anderson and Thomas F. Stransky (New York: Paulist Press; and Grand Rapids: Eerdmans, 1981), p. 266.

20. *The Validity of the Christian Mission,* p. 33.

21. Quoted by A. F. Carillo de Albernoz, *Roman Catholicism and Religious Liberty* (Geneva: World Council of Churches, 1959), p. 25.

22. *The Christian Message,* pp. 206, 45-6.

23. See Harvey T. Hoekstra, *The World Council of Churches and the Demise of Evangelism* (Wheaton, Illinois: Tyndale House, 1979).

24. "Mission and Humanization" (Ch. 1, n. 12), pp. 241, 243.

25. *Catholicism and Modernity* (Ch. 1, n. 9), p. 182.

26. "Theocratie en tolerantie (1966)," in *Theologisch werk* (Ch. 10, n. 30), Vol. III, p. 176.

27. *Pro Rege, of het Koningschap van Christus,* Vol. III (Kampen: J. H. Kok, 1912), p. 311; see also p. 582.

CHAPTER 12: INSTITUTIONAL IDENTITY

1. *Catholicism and Modernity* (Ch. 1, n. 9), p. 34.

2. Robert M. MacIver, *Academic Freedom in Our Time* (New York: Gordian Press, 1968), pp. 3-4.

3. Ralph F. Fuchs, "Academic Freedom—Its Basic Philosophy, Function, and History," in *Academic Freedom and Tenure: A Handbook of the American Association of University Professors,* ed. Louis Joughin (Madison, Milwaukee and London: University of Wisconsin Press, 1967), p. 242.

4. "You Can't Tell a School by Its Name," *Christianity Today* (Nov. 4, 1977), p. 21.

5. See MacIver, *Academic Freedom in Our Time,* pp. 285-9.

6. Quoted by Walter P. Metzger in *Academic Freedom in the Age of the University* (New York and London: Columbia University Press, 1961), p. 126.

7. *Heresy, Yes—Conspiracy, No* (Ch. 9, n. 13), p. 145.

8. See Peter Beyerhaus, "Mission and Humanization" (Ch. 1, n. 12), p. 239.

9. *A Letter Concerning Toleration* (Ch. 7, n. 15), pp. 7, 79.

10. *Agenda for Theology* (Introduction, n. 1), pp. 106-7.

11. *A Letter Concerning Toleration,* p. 29.

12. See Peter Hebblethwaite, *The New Inquisition? Schillebeeckx and Küng* (London: Collins, 1980), p. 43.

13. Article XVII, in *Creeds of the Churches* (Ch. 2, n. 8), pp. 306-7.

14. *Free Speech in the Church* (Westport, Connecticut: Greenwood

Press, 1981, reprint of the 1959 edition), p. 42.

15. "The Free Church Movement in Contemporary Catholicism," in *New Theology No. 6,* ed Martin E. Marty and Dean G. Peerman (New York: Macmillan; and London: Collier-Macmillan, 1969), pp. 273, 272.

16. "Is a New Christian Consensus Possible?" in *Consensus in Theology?* (Ch. 7, n. 1), pp. 65, 68.

17. *Free Speech in the Church,* pp. 36-7, 38.

18. *Tolerance* (Ch. 11, n. 5), p. 232.

19. *Agenda for Theology,* p. 96.

20. *Witch Hunt: The Revival of Heresy* (Boston: Little, Brown and Company, 1950), p. 306.

21. See MacIver, *Academic Freedom in Our Time,* p. 158.

22. Article XXVI, in *Creeds of the Churches,* p. 275.

CHAPTER 13: DOCTRINAL AND ACADEMIC FREEDOM

1. See "Areopagitica" (Ch. 6, n. 1), p. 35.

2. "Academic Freedom," in *Encyclopedia of the Social Sciences,* Vol. I (New York: Macmillan, 1937), p. 384.

3. "The Crisis of the University," in *In Defense of Academic Freedom,* ed. Sidney Hook (New York: Pegasus, 1971), pp. 103, 105.

4. *Academic Freedom in Our Time* (Ch. 12, n. 2), p. 17.

5. *Academic Freedom in Our Time*, p. 138.

6. *Academic Freedom in the Age of the University* (Ch. 12, n. 6), p. 92.

7. "Theology and the Reunion of the Churches," in *The Truth Is Concrete* (Ch. 1, n. 14), p. 29.

8. *Nieuwe wegen, oude sporen,* by J. H. Velema and W. H. Velema (Apeldoorn: Uitgeverij Semper Agendo, no date), p. 102.

9. *Eigentijdse verkondiging: Beschouwingen over de vertolking van het Evangelie in het taaleigen van de moderne mens* (Kampen: J. H. Kok, 1967), p. 88.

10. *Principles of Sacred Theology,* trans. J. Hendrik De Vries (Grand Rapids: Baker Book House, reprint of the 1898 edition), p. 593; see also p. 598.

11. *Principles of Sacred Theology,* pp. 588-9.

12. *Principles,* p. 591.

13. *Principles*, pp. 594, 596.

14. *The Protestant Era,* trans. James Luther Adams (Chicago: University of Chicago Press, 1948), pp. 165, xii, 163.

15. See the back section of the *Psalter Hymnal* (Ch. 10, n. 2), p. 19.

16. Quoted by Jerome J. Langford, *Galileo, Science and the Church,* revised edition (Ann Arbor: University of Michigan Press, 1971), p. 152.

17. *Galileo, Science and the Church,* p. 188.

18. *Does God Exist?* (Ch. 8, n. 15), p. 9.

19. *The Johns Hopkins University (1876-1891),* in *Johns Hopkins University Studies in Historical and Political Science* (Series IX), ed. Herbert Baxter Adams (Baltimore: The Johns Hopkins Press, 1891), p. 193.

20. "On Some Misconceptions Concerning Academic Freedom," in *Academic Freedom and Tenure* (Ch. 12, n. 3), p. 205.

21. See Shailer Mathews, *New Faith for Old* (Ch. 1, n. 7), p. 55.

22. "Academic Freedom and Professional Responsibilities," in *The Ethics of Teaching and Scientific Research,* ed. Sidney Hook, Paul Kurtz and Miro Todorovich (Buffalo: Prometheus Books, 1977), p. 118.

23. *On Christian Doctrine,* trans. D. W. Robertson, Jr. (Indianapolis and New York: Bobbs-Merrill, 1958), Book II, Chapter 40, Section 60, p. 75.

24. *On Being a Christian* (Ch. 1, n. 15), p. 430.

25. Quoted from the *Book of Confessions of the United Presbyterian Church in the United States of America,* second edition (Philadelphia: Office of the General Assembly of the United Presbyterian Church in the United States of America, 1970).

CHAPTER 14: THE PLACE OF APOLOGETICS

1. *A Passion for Truth: Hans Küng and His Theology* (New York: Crossroad, 1981), p. 260.

2. *Why Is Christianity True?* (Chicago: Winona Publishing, 1905), p. 4.

3. *Lectures on Calvinism* (Grand Rapids: Eerdmans, 1961, reprint of the 1931 edition), p. 11.

4. *Christianity and Liberalism* (Ch. 10, n. 29), pp. 7-8.

5. "On the History of the Psycho-Analytic Movement" (Ch. 8, nn. 3 and 5), p. 58.

6. "Apologetics and History," in *Life Is Religion* (Ch. 6, n. 15), p. 130.

7. See John Passmore, *A Hundred Years of Philosophy* (Harmondsworth, England: Penguin Books, 1968), p. 61.

8. See Leslie Stevenson, *Seven Theories of Human Nature* (New York and Oxford: Oxford University Press, 1974), p. 7.

9. *Ideology and the Ideologists* (New York, Evanston, San Francisco, and London: Harper and Row, 1975), p. 104.

10. *The Origins of Totalitarianism* (Cleveland and New York: World Publishing, 1958), p. 470.

11. *Gereformeerde Dogmatiek* (Ch. 8, n. 11), Vol. I, p. 482.

12. *E Voto Dordraceno* (Ch. 4, n. 4), Vol. IV, p. 334.

13. *Orthodoxy* (Ch. 2, n. 9), p. 19.

14. *Orthodoxy*, p. 28.

15. *Gereformeerde Dogmatiek,* Vol. I, pp. 479-80.

16. *A History of Apologetics* (Introduction, n. 11), p. xvi.

17. *Institutes* (Ch. 4, n. 8), Vol. I, p. 12; see also p. 9.

18. "Brunner as Apologist", in *The Theology of Emil Brunner,* ed. Charles W. Kegley (New York: Macmillan, 1962), pp. 292, 294.

19. "Brunner as Apologist," p. 296.

20. *Encyclopaedie der Heilige Godgeleerdheid*, revised edition, Vol. III (Kampen: J. H. Kok, 1909), p. 438.

21. *The Rebirth of Ministry: A Study of the Biblical Character of the Church's Ministry* (Philadelphia: Westminster Press, no date), p. 136.

22. "The Philosophy of Christian Evidences," in *Jerusalem and Athens: Critical Discussions on the Philosophy and Apologetics of Cornelius Van Til,* ed. E. R. Geehan (Nutley, N.J.: Presbyterian and Reformed Publishing Company, 1971), p. 425.

23. *Gereformeerde Dogmatiek,* Vol. I, p. 481; see also p. 33.

24. *The Certainty of Faith* (Ch. 10, n. 20), p. 22.

25. *The Interpretation of Religion* (Ch. 3, n. 8), p. 360.

26. *Progress of Dogma* (Ch. 2, n. 4), p. 38.

POSTSCRIPT: DO IDEAS MAKE A DIFFERENCE?

1. *Heroes and Heretics* (Ch. 9, n. 6), p. 347.

2. *Heresy, Yes—Conspiracy, No* (Ch. 9, n. 13), p. 73.

3. Quoted by MacIver, *Academic Freedom in Our Time* (Ch. 12, n. 2), p. 3.

4. James Drever, *A Dictionary of Psychology,* revised by Harvey Wallerstein (Baltimore: Penguin Books, 1964), p. 148.

5. *The Principles of Psychology,* Vol. II (New York: Dover Publications, 1950, reprint of the 1890 edition), pp. 449-50.

6. *The German Ideology,* ed. R. Pascal (New York: International Publishers, 1947), p. 15.

7. "Introduction," in *The Form of Ideology: Investigations into the Sense of Ideological Reasoning with a View to Giving an Account of Its Place in Political Life,* ed. D. J. Manning (London: George Allen & Unwin, 1980), p. 3.

8. "The Crime of Menticide," in *The American Journal of Psychiatry,* Vol. 107 (February 1951), p. 595; see also "Brainwashing and Menticide," in *Identity and Anxiety: Survival of the Person in Mass Society,* ed. Maurice Stein, Arthur J. Vidich and David Manning White (New York: Free Press, 1960), pp. 506-20.

9. See *The Rape of the Mind* (New York: Grosset & Dunlap, 1961), pp. 14, 96, 140, 149, 164, 240, 263, 281, 294ff.

10. *The Rape of the Mind,* p. 303.

11. See H. S. Holland, *The Apostolic Fathers* (London: S.P.C.K., no date), p. 194.

INDEX